GOD
IN THE
TRENCHES

A HISTORY OF HOW GOD DEFENDS
FREEDOM WHEN AMERICA IS AT WAR

ALSO BY LARKIN SPIVEY

*Miracles of the American Revolution: Divine Intervention and
the Birth of the Republic*
ISBN-13: 978-0-89957-021-1

Stories of Faith and Courage from World War II
(Battlefields and Blessings series)
ISBN-13: 978-0-89957-040-2

Coming in 2011:
Stories of Faith and Courage from the Vietnam War
(Battlefields and Blessings series)

GOD IN THE TRENCHES

A HISTORY OF HOW GOD DEFENDS FREEDOM WHEN AMERICA IS AT WAR

LARKIN SPIVEY

GOD & COUNTRY
PRESS

An Imprint of
AMG Publishers

DEDICATION

This book is dedicated to fellow Marines who didn't come home. I pray that God has a place of honor for these heroic young men who gave everything and had so little time in this world. I still feel close in spirit to my good friends Brad Collins, Judd Spainhour, Joe Loughran, and J. J. Carroll. I pay special homage to the courageous men of Kilo Company, Third Battalion, Third Marines: Raymond Macklin, Dale Carmichael, Michael Gibbs, Thomas Barrow, Lindy Hall, Patrick Gagnon, Charles Neal, Patrick Francisco, William Hedgpath, Leonard Laport, Ronald Lyvere, Stephen Nelson, Jeffery Maloney, William McCaskill, Kermit Ray, Rickey Southern, and Gary Newman. God bless each of these heroes and the loved ones who still have empty places in their hearts.

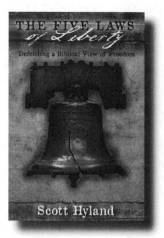
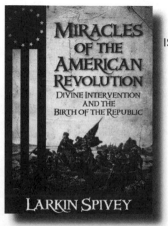

CONTENTS

LIST OF MAPS

ACKNOWLEDGMENTS

I WANT TO THANK Rick Steele and Dale Anderson of AMG Publishers for their vision in creating the God and Country imprint and for their confidence in me to be part of it. I also appreciate the guidance and support of David Sanford of Credo Communications. Much of the research for this book was accomplished at the U.S. Naval War College, where I benefited from the expertise of an outstanding library staff. I give special thanks to Michael Riggle and Alice Juda.

The love of my family has been the primary blessing of my life, and their support has been especially important during the process of creating this book. Anastasia, Bayliss, Catherine Alexa, and Windom have each in turn provided a unique viewpoint and influence on my thoughts. My wife, Lani, has been my partner in this as in everything else and has helped shape the scope and overall approach of this book at every stage.

Most significantly, I gratefully acknowledge the presence of Jesus Christ in my life and pray for his blessing on this work.

PREFACE

THIS BOOK is written for the skeptical reader. By that I mean someone who habitually doubts, questions, or disagrees. I believe that doubts and questions are very appropriate when a person is searching for something. The skeptic that I have in mind is searching for truth about life and for meaning in his own life and may be seeking answers in literature, science, philosophy, and even religion. This person may be open to the possibility of a spiritual life but has never had certain doubts resolved. He or she may have been turned off by some past experience with organized religion or with religious people who didn't seem able to live up to their own beliefs. The skeptic may question everything, but keeps looking for the truth. I know this person, because I have been him most of my life.

I would not be so presumptuous as to say that I know the truth about a lot of things now. In this book I try to present certain historical information that I have interpreted in light of my own religious beliefs. I have come to these beliefs somewhat late in my life and am still very conscious of my own skeptical attitudes. So, I am always cautious about trying too hard to convince another of anything. We all find our own truth in our own way. My way is outlined in the Appendix that I have provided for full disclosure of my background and my perspective in this work.

The recurring theme of this book is freedom. I believe the fact is obvious that America is great because her citizens are free. Countless Americans have fought and many have died to achieve and to preserve this condition. It is also my belief that God has blessed America because this freedom is very much in accordance with his plan for mankind. He has given men and women the free will to live their lives and to seek him or to turn away from him, each in accordance with his or her own conscience. Faith in God would be meaningless without this freedom.

I have written this book to show how I believe God has influenced the cause of freedom and the history of America at her most critical moments. It may be difficult to convince the skeptic that all of my conclusions are true. However, I expect that he or she will surely gain a sense of wonder at many of the seemingly miraculous events that have occurred at these critical times. I even hope to shake some assumptions about how effective many great leaders were in these events and to call into question how much control we have over every event in our own lives. If any of these realizations lead a skeptical reader to further thought and inquiry about the nature of God and his own relationship to God, I will be gratified.

Everyone of course isn't a skeptic. Atheists may not be persuaded to alter their beliefs about God by reading this book. Even so, I hope that they will read on and also wonder at some of the marvelous things that have occurred in the past and at how "lucky" America has been at many critical junctures. I also hope that many who read this book are Christians who already share many of the same underlying beliefs that shape my conclusions. I hope that they will find an affirmation of their faith through a fellow Christian's perspective on how God has worked and still works in the world.

I expect that some will be offended by my bringing the subjects of God and war together in one book, as if I am suggesting that God causes or looks favorably on war. What a Christian's attitude about war should be is a complicated question which I am not qualified to fully address. Theologians have tied themselves in knots trying to condemn violence in general and to justify certain wars in particular. Jesus said simply, "Love your enemies and pray for those that persecute you."[1] If mankind could absorb this lesson there would not be any wars. If Christians' actions were consistent with their beliefs there should at least be no wars between "Christian" nations. Unfortunately, such wars have occurred repeatedly in history. Christians and the rest of mankind are far from perfect. A wise man once said, "Only the dead have seen the end of war." This would seem to be an unfortunate but valid observation.

In 1944, at the height of World War II, Archbishop (at that time) Francis Spellman wrote about the American soldier:

> He and millions of his generation who were living useful, peaceful lives, suddenly saw the massing of the clouds of war. America's future and greatness were in danger. They must be protected and preserved! And so, he became a soldier. Life went into complete reverse! It became a turmoil, dedicated to and consumed with the spirit of destruction. That he might defend and save, he was taught to attack and destroy.[2]

Cardinal Spellman may have later modified his thoughts about war, but these words were written while confronting the reality of a threat to America's existence and with faith in God's protection. His words brought consolation and faith to millions facing the uncertainty of war and survival. There shouldn't have been a war, but that issue was not in his hands.

In light of what we know about history, I believe that it is necessary to be prepared for war. I believe that God blesses our efforts to protect ourselves, especially when these efforts lead to avoiding conflict. My outlook is undoubtedly colored by my career in military service. I have considered self-defense and military preparedness to be a high calling for so long that I probably have difficulty with the simplicity of Christ's own words. When military conflicts have occurred, I do believe that God has been disappointed. Even during times of war, however, I believe that God continues to exert his influence over events in accordance with his own plans. The purpose of this book is to show evidence of how he may have done this in the past.

I have sought God's blessing of my efforts in writing this book and have prayed constantly for his guidance. I have also prayed for forgiveness if I have reached too far in speculating about his purposes. At this point I can only hope that he has given me some insight and that I have received his guidance during the normal process of my own studying and thinking. There have been exciting moments when I seemed to gain new insights into subjects that I had been studying and when random thoughts seemed to come together in my mind to form a clearer picture. At times the words and paragraphs seemed to flow onto the paper. Still, I can only assert that these are my own thoughts and words and hope that God has been involved and has somehow looked favorably on my effort.

The lot is cast into the lap, but its every decision is from the Lord.

—PROVERBS 16:33

CHAPTER ONE

PURE LUCK OR GOD'S HAND?

I HAD NEVER BEEN *so scared. The mortar attack seemed to go on for hours, although I would learn later that it lasted only minutes. The air was filled with smoke, dirt, and shrapnel. I could feel the shock wave of each exploding mortar shell as I lay exposed on open ground. I had been caught without a foxhole or even an entrenching tool and quickly noticed that no one else was so ill prepared. I had flown in by helicopter to join Third Battalion, Third Marines the day before, on March 24, 1967. At first light the next morning I learned that infantry battalion command groups were favorite targets of North Vietnamese mortar teams. With no duties to perform, all that I could do was think about where the next shell was going to land and pray that it wouldn't be on top of me. I did pray, and I did survive that attack, as well as other close calls during my time in the Vietnam War and during my career as a Marine infantry officer. For most of my life I have not been a religious person, but have still had to deal with a recurring question: Have I been an extremely*

*lucky man, or has God's hand protected me during many dangerous
and pivotal moments?*

APPARENT LUCK

The subject of luck has always intrigued me. It is natural to feel
lucky after coming unscathed through a close call, and I have felt
that way many times. During my combat tour in Vietnam, I was
actually possessed with the idea that I had a finite amount of luck
to draw on. Each time that I came under fire, I felt afterward that
I had used a little more of my allotted quota. At times, my account
seemed to get pretty low. On one occasion, as my company was
about to depart on an operation, one of my troops refused to go,
telling me that he felt unlucky and that something bad was going
to happen. Since I wasn't able to deal with his problem at that
moment, I sent him back to a rear area. He was killed that night
by a direct hit from a rare rocket attack on our base at Dong Ha.
This unsettling incident contributed to my superstitious outlook
at the time, making me worry about coming to a similar state of
mind. On another occasion a fellow airline passenger turned to
me and told me how nervous he was. I told him not to worry, that
nothing would happen to him until his time was up. His response
was, "That may be true, but I don't want to be on the flight when
your time is up!" Moments such as these subtly framed the question of chance versus design in my own life.

As a student of military history, I have also been aware of incidents in war where the outcome of battles seemed to hang on luck.
At these times the opposing forces were arrayed against each other
as the commanders deployed their units and set events into motion.
Communications and logistics were planned in detail. Small unit
leaders executed their orders as men fought and in many cases died.
The outcomes of these battles and wars are now well recorded in

history and have a certain inevitability about them, as does all of history in retrospect. We know that America won her independence, the South lost the Civil War, and the Allies were victorious in World War II. How could it have been otherwise? The great leaders and great resources of the victorious powers were brought to bear and the events unfolded as we now know they were meant to. For most of my life I never questioned in my own mind the inevitability of these historical events. I have seen it as a simple curiosity that luck seemed to play a role in war, even at times a large role. It was merely an interesting novelty to me that great events often depended on small, apparently random circumstances.

Many great thinkers seem comfortable with the concept of luck and its importance to history and science. Many cosmologists believe that random patterns of events led to the creation of the universe and of life itself. Discussing evolution and extinction, Harvard paleontologist Stephen Jay Gould uses a random model in which "species live or die by the roll of the dice and the luck of the draw."[3] Bertrand Russell viewed man as an "accidental collection of atoms."[4] Quantum physicists argue that the nature of matter itself is explained by mathematical probabilities. Einstein was troubled by this aspect of what was then the "new physics" and said that, "God does not play dice,"[5] giving evidence of a belief that there is more than luck at work in the design of the universe.

I have allowed Einstein to introduce the subject of God at this point. I intend to take the existence of God for granted as a matter of my own faith, as explained in the Appendix. I believe that most would agree with this assumption, even though views on the character and nature of God would vary over a vast spectrum. The key question relevant here is: Does God actively interact with humanity? It is my own belief that he does and that he has been active throughout history in carrying out his own purpose for mankind. I have come to believe less in luck and more in the fulfillment of that purpose. I will cite other support for this view in Chapter Six. The historical information and opinions that will be presented are intended to support this view and to challenge readers who might have some other interpretation of how or why these well-documented events happened.

THE HAND OF PROVIDENCE

Seeking God's role in historical events has been a challenging task. My focus has been on those military situations where luck apparently played a key role in the outcome. I believe that God's providential hand can be seen in these details of history. When I found many of these occurrences surrounding critical battles and possible turning points in these wars, I was led to wonder about God's larger purpose on these occasions. Why would he have intervened at these times? After studying these events and considering these questions, I have proposed some answers that make sense to me. Proof is of course not possible. My fundamental belief is that God is good and that he has worked for the good in history. Sometimes this good is readily apparent. Sometimes it is not discernible at all from our perspective. Perhaps it is enough for us to learn simply that we are not always in control. We do our best to organize, direct, and take charge. We struggle to exert our influence on events. In spite of all these efforts, God seems to have the final word. Although he often works in ways that we don't understand, there are times when his influence is more apparent. The events addressed in this book will present some of those times when we can see God's hand at work.

I don't enter into speculation about God's purposes and plans lightly. When Job went too far in questioning God, God reprimanded him from the whirlwind, saying:

Who is this that darkens my counsel with words without knowledge? Brace yourself like a man; I will question you, and you shall answer me. Where were you when I laid the earth's foundation? Tell me, if you understand. Who marked off its dimensions? Surely you know! Who stretched a measuring line across it? On what were its footings set, or who laid its cornerstone—while the morning stars sang together and all the angels shouted for joy?[6]

I believe that God was telling Job and all mankind that the full breadth and majesty of his infinite creation and his plans for it are too vast to be comprehended. He has revealed certain aspects of himself and his designs to individuals over the course of history, giving us pieces of information and the Bible as a reference. I believe that when we study this information we are led to believe that God works for the good in history and in the lives of individuals, even though sometimes this good is hard to understand. Bad things do happen. It is beyond my scope to present Christian theology in any area, least of all in regard to the presence of evil in the world. For his own reason, God made the world and then made man and woman in his own image. He gave them free will to act, to think, and even to believe whatever they want. Although our highest purpose is to seek God's will through a relationship with him, he compels none to do so. Many try to do good and try to please God and still fall short. Many others totally ignore or deny God and pursue their own ends. For his own reasons and in accordance with his own design he did not place us on earth to be directly subordinated to his will. I believe that in his own way and in his own time God is on the side of the good even as he allows people to do bad things or allows bad things to happen. Often these bad things are nothing more than nature taking its course. It is obviously not easy to discern how God works in the world, and

I am conscious of the pitfalls of assuming too much and of reaching too far. Still, I believe that it is possible to find some events in history where we can see God's hand at work and even the fulfillment of his purpose.

CRITICAL TIMES IN AMERICA'S HISTORY

In looking at American history we can see a number of wartime situations where the nation's survival or at least its form of existence was in doubt. The Revolutionary War, the Civil War, World War II, and one moment in the Cold War are clearly in this category. If the Revolutionary War had taken a different turn, the United States of America would have been stillborn. England would have consolidated her position of authority and control in North America. History would have been written differently. If the South had prevailed during the Civil War, who can guess at the long-range result? Perhaps, with a clearly established right of secession, we would still be in a process of subdividing our separate nations. It is especially difficult to imagine the consequences of American defeat during World War II. Although this may never have been likely, at one time there was a distinct possibility that Germany would prevail in Europe and Japan in the Pacific. How would the world look today? And finally, the Cuban Missile Crisis brought us to the climax of the Cold War, where we actually came face-to-face with an all-out nuclear war and devastation of the planet.

These wars will be examined in enough depth to understand what happened generally and to understand the relationship of the political, diplomatic, religious, and military aspects. Everything presented leads to the critical point of each war. In each case the critical point seemed to come early in the conflict. When we put ourselves back in time, we see better the uncertainty of events as they unfolded. Early in each of these wars uncertainty was rampant. Antiwar sentiment was strong and carried more weight in America than in most other countries due to American democratic traditions. Early disasters had more potential for serious political consequences. Early disasters did occur or came extremely close to occurring in each of these wars. Amazingly, miraculous things seemed to happen repeatedly at these critical points. It is my purpose to suggest that these occurrences were not the luck of the draw, but were manifestations of God at work in America's history toward the fulfillment of his own plan.

AMERICA'S PLACE IN GOD'S PLAN

In looking at the history of Christianity, it is not difficult to see that America has had a special place in God's plan for mankind. By the 1600s the powers of church and state were joined fast throughout most of Europe in Catholic as well as Protestant countries. In a broad sense a level of stagnation had grown within these churches where an all-powerful clergy ruled, the laity had little voice, and the forms of worship and membership were compelled by the state. For hundreds of years throughout Europe every member of society was generally assumed to automatically be a member of the established church within a country. The early colonies in America provided a safety valve for groups of worshippers unable to live and grow spiritually under these conditions. A group of Calvinist separatists came to Plymouth via Holland in 1620 as pilgrims to a New Jerusalem. They were followed by waves of Puritans fleeing official church repression in England during the 1630s and '40s. The Second Lord Baltimore established Maryland in 1634 with specific guarantees of religious toleration, at first attracting Catholics, and then a variety of other Christian groups. William Penn founded Pennsylvania in 1681 as a "holy experiment" and haven for all forms of religion, attracting large numbers of Quakers and other minority Christian groups from many European countries.

Many members of the Church of England, or Anglicans, came to America, including the original Puritans, but found that time and distance from England molded their churches into the patterns being established all around them. There was little or no effective central authority. The facilities were spartan and the services simple. A strong laity grew up with a powerful interest in church governance. The rapidly growing diversity thwarted most attempts to organize whole communities under one church. The concept of the gathered church took hold, where each church had to attract and hold its own congregation. Evangelism and individual conversion grew in significance. The individual's relationship to God became more of the focal point of church activity.[7] In many respects many of these colonial churches resembled the very earliest gatherings of Christian worshippers. Many new world Christians had a renewed sense of urgency and mission about their religion. Although many of these new churches would eventually become organized, I believe that this fresh start for the church was blessed by God and in accordance with his plans. I believe that the underlying theme was freedom, freedom to come to God or not. Only with this freedom is faith meaningful in God's sight. I believe that a fundamental prerequisite of this freedom to worship is a political freedom that leaves more initiative and responsibility to the individual. As we will see in Chapter Two, conditions for this political freedom came to exist in the English colonies in the 1700s. As I see it, this was in accordance with God's purpose and was the basis for America's special place in God's plan for mankind. America clearly has maintained this special place throughout much of her history, as I hope to show in Chapters Three, Four, and Five. Whether she continues today or for how long she will continue in the future are questions that will be considered in Chapter Six.

It is for freedom that Christ has set us free.

—GALATIANS 5:1

CHAPTER TWO

THE AMERICAN REVOLUTION— DARKEST HOUR

I N DECEMBER 1776 *the phrase "Revolutionary War" would have seemed overly grandiose to describe what was happening in the American colonies. There was indeed an armed conflict in progress. In late August a British army of over 30,000 troops under General William Howe had landed in New York to quell an "uprising." Opposing Howe were an assortment of local militia units from various colonies now under the command of George Washington, a newly appointed general with little experience. Howe's army of British regulars and Hessian mercenaries did its work efficiently. The rebels were routed out of New York and pursued and depleted across New Jersey. The loyalists throughout the state began rallying to the winning side. By December, Washington had pulled the remnant of his beaten force across the Delaware River, leaving all of New Jersey to the British. By January most of his few remaining troops would see their one-year enlistments expire. Also by then the river would be frozen allowing Howe's forces to continue the advance on Philadelphia, which the colonial congress had already evacuated. The rebellion was about to be over. In this last desperate hour, Washington conceived a plan that at best could be considered a pure gamble. He would recross the Delaware and strike the Hessian garrison at Trenton. He would risk what was left of his army by taking this last chance to turn the tide. He was doing what he thought he had to do, but was in fact unknowingly placing his own fate and that of an uncertain nation in the hand of God.*

POLITICS IN ENGLAND

Trouble in the American colonies had been simmering for many years in reaction mainly to political developments in England. Although English history over the centuries has been centered on its kings and queens, by the late 1600s political parties had begun to come into being. The Whigs generally favored a greater role of Parliament in governing, whereas the Tories favored more power to the king and church.

In the early 1700s, Whig influence became dominant under George I, a German who spoke no English and who had been called to the throne by Parliament in the belief that he would exercise little royal power. George I was followed by the similar George II. Under these monarchs the real power was exercised by Sir Robert Walpole, considered England's first prime minister, and a Whig dominated Parliament. Walpole followed a policy toward the American colonies of benign neglect, allowing a great degree of self-governance and little interference from London. In 1760 the young George III came to the throne at age twenty-two. He had been raised in England and was resolved to restore Tory power to the English throne. There followed a period of turmoil within the government as the king selected ministers loyal to himself and sought to realign Parliament in his favor. His administration also resolved to reassert control over the colonies.

By the mid-1700s the concept of representative government and a constrained monarchy were well advanced in England compared to any other nation of the time. However, only certain select elements of the society were "represented." The nobility and landowning classes were dominant. The wealthy merchants and commercial interests were growing in power. Political consideration of the common people of England was practically nonexistent. The steady progress of the industrial revolution was bringing more and more people into the factory system as ordinary laborers. The Enclosure Acts virtually eliminated common lands and the opportunity for independent farming, reducing many to the status of wage earners for the large landowners. A great mass of humanity was growing that had more in common with the colonists in America than with their own government.

RIVALRY BETWEEN ENGLAND AND FRANCE

From 1688 until 1763, England was almost constantly at war in Europe, usually against France. Animosity developed from a fierce competition for influence and trade worldwide. This competition repeatedly spilled over into conflicts between English and French settlers in America. The French did not develop colonies to the extent of the English, but did range far over Canada and areas to the west of the English colonies exploring, hunting, and establishing trading posts. The most serious confrontation started in 1754 when George Washington was sent by the governor of Virginia to challenge the establishment of French outposts along the Allegheny River in what is now western Pennsylvania. Washington's force was defeated in what was to be the first battle of a long war. This time the conflict was to spill over into Europe and would lead to the Seven Years' War or what Winston Churchill called the "First World War."[8]

The Seven Years' War started in 1756 with a complete realignment of European alliances. England and Prussia joined forces against France, Austria, and Russia. Prussia and Austria fought for control of central Europe, while England and France battled for supremacy on the seas and in North America and India. After several years with little success, a cabinet reshuffle was accomplished in England with William Pitt coming to power as the secretary of state with almost unlimited war powers. Pitt proved to be one of history's most successful commanders-in-chief. He orchestrated English forces worldwide to capitalize on her strengths. He gave token assistance to Frederick of Prussia for operations in Europe while focusing his power at sea on objectives that would enhance England's position as a trading nation. He bottled up the French fleet at Brest and Toulon and undertook successful campaigns in Canada, India, and the West Indies. Spain belatedly entered the war in 1762 giving Pitt the opportunity to seize Cuba and the Philippines. The Peace of Paris in 1763 recognized England's dominant position worldwide. France ceded Canada and all territory east of the Mississippi River. Florida was received from Spain in exchange for Cuba.

The conclusion of the Seven Years' War brought peace for the first time to the frontier of the American colonies. The colonists were relieved and grateful to England for her success and protection. Of course the royal treasury had paid the bills and British soldiers had done most of the fighting. This fact was well known in Parliament and generally ignored in the colonies, a condition that was to prove troublesome in the near future. British officers were generally unimpressed with the colonial militia units that they occasionally employed, coloring their judgment of what were to be future adversaries. The successful conclusion of war brought a period of apparent tranquility to the British Empire. Unfortunately it also brought an opportunity to focus on some lingering problems with the colonies in America. Elimination of the French threat on the frontier also eliminated a significant aspect of the colonies' dependence on England.

POLITICS IN THE COLONIES

To finance this very lengthy war England had amassed a huge debt of nearly £130.[9] To compound this problem a serious economic slump followed the war with bad harvests, rising prices, and industrial disputes.[10] The acquisition of Canada and new lands to the west of the colonies would require garrisons totaling as many as ten thousand regular troops. Such a military presence would cost an estimated two hundred thousand pounds per year.[11] As to who should pay this bill, it was obvious to George III and Parliament—the American colonies themselves. From 1764 to 1773 a series of taxes on colonial goods and services were enacted in England. Each new measure brought a new crisis and stiffening resistance from the colonies. In America the issue became taxation without representation. In England the issue became obedience to authority. The resulting strains over this decade began to forge a semblance of unity among the colonies.

Considering the disparate peoples and interests of the American colonies, any degree of unity was almost miraculous. Each colony had a unique history of its own, with separate governments, unique commercial interests, and differing cultural and religious backgrounds. Loyalty to the Crown ran deep everywhere. Particularly in the South, the agricultural economy was almost totally dependent on trade with England. Much of the growing crisis centered on one area, Boston. When a group of dissidents dumped tea into Boston harbor in December 1773,

Parliament reacted by passing the Coercive Acts (called the Intolerable Acts in the colonies), closing Boston harbor and suspending the Massachusetts Assembly. This massive retribution against Massachusetts was aimed at setting an example and at dividing the colonies. With Boston's port closed, a sizable redistribution of trade to other ports was in order. In England it was expected that the other colonies would seize this opportunity. The opposite occurred. Boston received an outpouring of financial and logistic support from many other areas and from as far away as South Carolina. Soon, a call came from Virginia for a meeting in Philadelphia with representatives from every colony.[12]

CONTINENTAL CONGRESS

Fifty-six delegates representing every colony except Georgia assembled in Carpenters Hall in Philadelphia on September 5, 1774. Episcopal, Lutheran, Roman Catholic, Presbyterian, and other church bells tolled in greeting.[13] The full extent of colonial diversity was evident. Lawyers, doctors, merchants, farmers, loyalists, radicals, middle-of-the-roaders, and most religious denominations were all represented. One early matter settled agreeably was to open each session in prayer. This occurred when Samuel Adams, a Congregationalist, nominated the Reverend Duche, an Episcopalian, to be chaplain of the assembly.[14] Other issues weren't so easy. Over the course of fifty-one days, the delegates attempted to reach agreement on the question of colonial rights and of what to do in response to British oppression. The conservative or loyalist side favored conciliation. The radical side favored vigorous opposition. All were afraid of war and the probability of absolute despotism if a war were started and lost. Feelings of loyalty to the Crown were strong, even though most were adamantly opposed to Parliament's actions.

Finally the first Continental Congress came to some firm but generally moderate conclusions. The Intolerable Acts and acts taxing the colonies were condemned. A boycott of British imports and exports was agreed pending repeal of those acts, with certain exceptions for South Carolina and Virginia. A direct appeal to King George was drafted asking for his intervention and assuring him that his royal authority would be maintained. Some hoped that the king might restore reasonable governance and rectify the wrongs that many perceived had been inflicted by Parliament.

Unfortunately, it was the new king himself leading the way toward a hardening of British attitudes. His agenda was to reestablish royal power. He made no response to the colonial congress. This would have tended to give recognition to their legal standing. He showed no apparent interest or understanding of what was happening in Philadelphia. He called his ministers to a new level of firmness and resolve toward the colonies. This policy was opposed by Whig elements in Parliament, but was well received by the king's supporters who were obsessed with budget deficits and an attitude that the colonies existed only for the benefit of England.[15] Early in 1775 General Gage, commanding the British garrison in Boston, received his orders from London. He was to use force in dealing with the rebellion.

Throughout New England local militia units were preparing themselves to resist the growing threat of British troops being used to carry out Parliament's edicts. These citizen-soldiers trained to respond on short notice and called themselves "Minutemen." On April 19, 1775, Gage sent a force of 700 out of Boston to seize military stores at Concord and to capture rebel leaders in Lexington. The Minutemen mobilized to oppose this expedition. In a confrontation at Lexington, shots were fired resulting in eight dead colonials. A sharp engagement followed on the outskirts of

Concord at North Bridge. The British force fell back toward Boston under fire most of the way. Within a few days militia units from throughout the region began assembling around Boston. Loyalists from surrounding areas began flooding into the city for protection. The militia units had apparently achieved the upper hand as an uneasy standoff took shape.

SECOND CONTINENTAL CONGRESS

On May 10, 1775, the Continental Congress reconvened in Philadelphia in an atmosphere of crisis. Militia units were organizing throughout the colonies. Blood had been shed in Massachusetts. There was general anger and almost war fever evident among many of the delegates. The loyalist factions were subdued but not inactive. Caution was urged. Some asserted the opinion that the conflict was a New England problem alone. What became known as the Olive Branch Petition was approved and sent to the king asking for reconciliation and an end to hostilities. Although armed conflict seemed likely, there was little agreement as to the end result. Most continued to hope for a redress of grievances and a return to normalcy. A few began to consider the idea of independence. In spite of its official position favoring reconciliation, the Congress took steps to assume powers of a sovereign authority. In effect, a government was formed with power in the Congress to make peace or war and to regulate commerce. Internal affairs were left to each colony.

From the Massachusetts Provincial Congress came a plea that could not be ignored. A colonial army was needed to face the British. The New England troops around Boston were offered as a nucleus. After weeks of debate a vote was passed on June 14 to establish a Continental army. The next day forty-three-year-old George Washington was voted commander-in-chief. To finance

Portrait of General George Washington. (National Archives)

this effort, a three million dollar issue of United Colony currency was approved backed by the faith of the Congress. Washington departed within days to take command of the new army and situation around Boston.

MILITARY ACTIONS IN NEW ENGLAND

At about the same time that General Washington set out for Massachusetts, a detachment of colonial troops under Colonel William Prescott occupied Breed's Hill overlooking Boston from the north (Bunker's Hill was nearby but not the scene of the action). General Gage, the British commander in Boston, immediately recognized the tactical significance of this move and responded with an attack to clear the hill. The rebel troops fought off two assaults, inflicting severe casualties on the British regulars. Running out of ammunition, they were finally forced off the position. The British commanders were again shocked by the effectiveness of this colonial 'rabble' opposing their best troops. Washington arrived on July 2 to take command of what was now the Continental army and to take charge of what was becoming the siege of Boston.

Faced with the problems of molding a group of militia units into an army, Washington maintained the cordon around Boston during the fall and winter of 1775. The enlistments of a large number of troops expired on December 31. An army had to be built almost from scratch within musket range of the enemy. By the time Henry Knox arrived with over fifty artillery pieces sledded overland from the recently captured Fort Ticonderoga, Washington was finally ready for offensive action. During the evening of March 4, 1776, Dorchester Heights was occupied giving the Continental forces a commanding position facing the city from the south over Boston harbor. Faced with another Breed's Hill situation made worse by the presence of artillery, General Howe, the new British commander, prepared a waterborne assault across the harbor to clear the heights. Twenty-five hundred troops were embarked in transports for the attack when a violent storm came up, referred to by the locals as a "hurrycane."[17] The troops could not be landed, and the attack had to be postponed. Washington continued strengthening his positions until Howe realized he was too late. His position had become untenable. Boston was evacuated on March 17. Morale soared as news of this great victory swept through the colonies. General Washington knew that he had little time to celebrate.

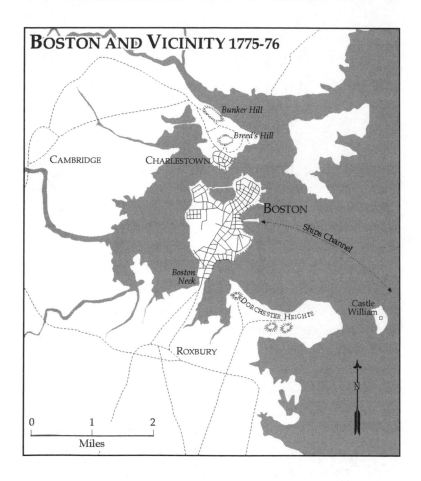

DECLARATION OF INDEPENDENCE

By mid-August 1775, the Olive Branch Petition passed by the second Continental Congress reached London. Since the Crown did not recognize the legitimacy of the Congress, the petition was not addressed. Instead, on August 23 a Proclamation of Rebellion was issued, in effect declaring that England and the colonies were in a state of war.[18] Although actions around Boston confirmed

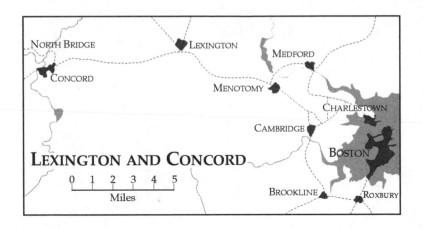

that war seemed to be starting, there continued to be no agreement in the Congress as to the long-term goal. Most continued
hoping for reconciliation and a return to normalcy. However, as
1776 wore on, sentiment on this issue began to shift. As the British gave up Boston, a wave of optimism grew among the representatives. Reports began coming in of the British hiring mercenaries
to fight in America.[19] In May the assemblies of Massachusetts and
Virginia voted for independence. Focused debate on the question
of independence began in Congress on July 1. John Adams called
this the "greatest debate of all." That day nine states voted for independence. On July 2 twelve states voted in favor, with only New
York abstaining. A new nation was born.

A committee had been formed to put into writing what the
representatives approved. Benjamin Franklin, John Adams, Roger
Sherman, Robert Livingston, and Thomas Jefferson presented the
immortal proclamation:

> We hold these truths to be self-evident, that all men are cre-
> ated equal, that they are endowed by their Creator with certain

inalienable Rights, that among these are Life, Liberty, and the
pursuit of Happiness.... And for the support of this Declaration,
with a firm reliance on the protection of divine Providence, we
mutually pledge to each other our Lives, our Fortunes, and our
sacred Honor.[20]

On July 4, 1776, the Declaration of Independence was formally
ratified and individually signed by each of the fifty-six delegates.
Responsibility for their actions could never be denied. The legitimacy of the new nation would go beyond colonial assemblies, gov-
ernors, Parliament, and any royal authority. The United States of
America would be under the authority and protection of God and
based on God-given rights. Samuel Adams rose in the assembly to
state, "We have this day restored the Sovereign, to Whom alone
men ought to be obedient."

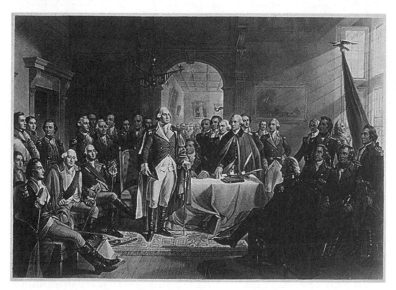

Washington and His Generals. (National Archives)

MILITARY ACTIONS IN NEW YORK
AND NEW JERSEY

Almost at the same time that the Declaration of Independence was being signed, a fleet of British ships appeared in New York harbor. Within a few weeks General Howe had over thirty thousand regular British and Hessian mercenary troops on hand and a fleet of over four hundred warships and transports. In the months following the occupation of Boston, Washington had correctly concluded that this was where Howe would strike. By taking New York and patrolling the Hudson River, Howe could isolate New England and split the colonies. Gradually Washington's forces had increased to almost twenty thousand men with many of his same New England units and newly organized militia units from other colonies. For weeks their time had been spent digging in and preparing defensive positions. Under pressure from Congress,

Washington had unwisely decided to defend Long Island and Manhattan, both areas that could be flanked and bypassed by British ships. On August 22, 1776, the methodical Howe began his campaign by landing troops on Long Island. Intent on avoiding another Breed's Hill, he smartly enveloped Washington's position striking his left flank and rear. The colonials were routed in these first clashes and fell back to stronger positions on Brooklyn Heights. As weather permitted Howe began building up his forces and extending trenches toward the American positions. He tried to move warships up the East River to disrupt Washington's supplies and to bring his positions under fire from the rear, but a strong storm with northeast winds made this ship movement impossible during the brief period when it could have been decisive.[21]

It finally became apparent to Washington that his position on Long Island was untenable and that he was in danger of losing a major portion of his army. But now he had enemy troops closely engaged to his front and the broad expanse of the East River to his rear. Fortunately, one of his units on Long Island was John Glover's 14th Massachusetts Regiment composed of seamen from that state's Marblehead area. Washington turned to Glover to get his men off Long Island. During the evening of August 29 this revolutionary era version of Dunkirk (the 1940 evacuation of the British army from France) was miraculously accomplished. Using a random collection of small craft gathered from the local area, Glover's men ferried Washington's army of 9,500 men across the East River. The two-mile round trip was repeated over and over throughout the night. At any moment if Howe's men had figured out what was in progress, disaster would have resulted. As dawn began to break, the exodus was still not complete. At this moment a fog began to rise off the East River that completely screened the final trips over several more morning hours. Finally, in one of the last boats, the commander-in-chief himself embarked. Washington and his army had escaped a total disaster.[22]

The military situation did not improve for the colonial forces on Manhattan. Howe moved with extreme caution always seeking to avoid frontal assaults on prepared positions. He used his ships to bypass strongpoints, moving up the Hudson and East rivers. By October 16 Washington was forced to abandon Manhattan. He retreated north toward Westchester and tried to establish another defensive line at White Plains. On the 28th Howe turned this position with another flanking movement, again coming close to destroying the Continental army. On November 16 the British captured Fort Washington on the Hudson River, taking almost three thousand prisoners. Constantly guessing at Howe's intentions, Washington divided his forces, leaving 5,500 troops under Gen. Charles Lee north of New York City to guard the main routes into New England. With the remainder of his forces, he

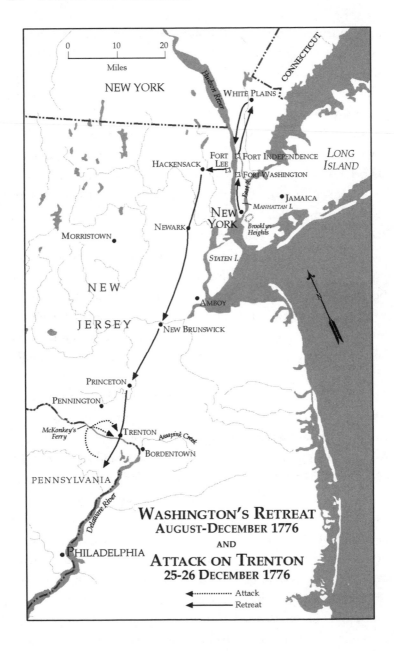

WASHINGTON'S RETREAT
AUGUST-DECEMBER 1776
AND
ATTACK ON TRENTON
25-26 DECEMBER 1776

crossed the Hudson into New Jersey to defend against a thrust to the south and Philadelphia.

DARKEST HOUR

Washington immediately found himself faced by a well-equipped army of 10,000 British and Hessian troops under the command of Gen. Charles Cornwallis. Washington's army was now plagued with desertions and expiring enlistments. On November 30 almost 2,000 militiamen from New Jersey and Maryland left the ranks. The defense of New Jersey turned into an escalating retreat through Hackensack, Newark, and Brunswick. By December the colonials were at Trenton on the Delaware River with about 3,000 men remaining in ranks. Most of these looked forward to expiring enlistments at the end of the year. Washington wrote to his brother Augustine, " If every nerve is not strained to recruit the new army with all possible expedition, I think the game is pretty nearly up. . . . You can form no idea of the perplexity of my situation. No man, I believe, ever had a greater choice of difficulties, and less means to extricate himself from them."[23] Washington was about out of men and materiel. His supply situation was pitiful. Uniforms were nonexistent, and men had to wear whatever they could find to cover their bodies and feet, which wasn't much. Sickness began to prey on exhausted, underfed, exposed, and demoralized troops. With Washington's army at this time was the writer Thomas Paine. At this point in the campaign he wrote the pamphlet "The American Crisis," which began, "These are the times that try men's souls. The summer soldier and sunshine patriot will, in this crisis, shrink from the service of his country; but he that stands it now, deserves the love and thanks of every man and woman." In spite of Paine's eloquence, soldiers continued to disappear from the ranks.

As Washington pulled his tattered army back across the Delaware on December 7 the new nation had quickly come to its darkest hour. The euphoria of the summer had given way to despair over the collapsing military situation. The British invasion force had taken on an aura of invincibility. Nothing lay between it and Philadelphia except a rapidly disappearing army and a river that was already beginning to freeze over and would soon be no obstacle to advancing troops. The political repercussions began to multiply. Feeling unsafe in Philadelphia, the Congress moved to Baltimore. Voices were heard criticizing General Washington for his failure to make a stand. Rumors circulated of a move to replace him with General Lee. Behind the advancing British lines loyalist sentiment was growing throughout New Jersey and New York. General Howe had encouraged this trend by issuing a proclamation of pardon on November 30 to all who would swear allegiance to the king. Thousands took advantage of the offer.[24] It seemed that the thirteen states were about to become twelve or even eleven. As Washington was being criticized, Howe was promoted to full general and knighted by King George in recognition of his achievements.

For weeks General Washington had implored Charles Lee to rejoin the main army with the force assigned to him. Lee delayed and resisted complying with this order, as he had ambitions of his own to take over command of the Continental army. His correspondence revealed a growing disdain for Washington's leadership. Then, in a peculiar and embarrassing incident Lee was captured by British dragoons while at a tavern several miles from his command on December 13. This coup was met with rejoicing among the British and viewed as a disaster by most Americans who considered Lee one of the few experienced officers in the army. The loss of Washington's second in command fueled the already growing panic in the Congress and gave the British cause for further confidence in the military situation. However, this incident was more correctly termed by one historian as the 'Luckiest Friday the Thirteenth in History.'[25] The immediate beneficial result was to remove a growing and misguided challenge to Washington's authority and to see Lee's 2000 troops speedily returned to Washington's control by General John Sullivan. As other reinforcements began to arrive, Washington was able for the first time to at least consider the possibility of offensive action.

By December 22 Washington had begun to finalize a plan to recross the Delaware and to attack the Hessian garrison occupying Trenton. The Hessian brigade at Trenton consisted of three regiments of 1,400 veteran troops commanded by Colonel Johann Rall. Rall's Hessians had fought at Fort Washington and had accepted the surrender of the American forces captured there six weeks before. By the time they occupied Trenton, Colonel Rall and his troops were very high in self-confidence and quite low in their opinion of the Continental army.

Washington's plan called for a force of 2,400 men under his own command to cross the river on Christmas night at McKonkey's Ferry, nine miles north of the town, and to strike Trenton before first light. This was not an overwhelming force to throw against a defended position. Most commanders would consider a numerical advantage of three to one barely adequate in such an attack. Washington had to rely on complete and total surprise for any chance of success. He was counting on Christmas celebrations and darkness. He got unexpected help from some of the worst weather on record that added a degree of safety, along with untold misery, to the venture. Even so, any warning or any degree of alertness among the Hessians would have spelled total disaster. The odds were decidedly against Washington as he took what can only be considered a desperate gamble. Although he used all the resources available and planned this action to the best of his ability, the outcome was not in his control. God's hand would be the critical factor at Washington's most desperate moment.

THE "PHANTOM ATTACK"

Since arriving in Trenton on December 12, Colonel Rall and his Hessian force had been busy. It was Rall's intention to cross the river as soon as it was frozen and to move against Philadelphia.[26] While in Trenton, however, he had to focus considerable energy on maintaining his lines of communication against small bands of rebels appearing east of the Delaware. He sent patrols out from Trenton, several of which encountered and exchanged fire with colonials. His immediate superior, Col. Von Donop, was concerned with this activity and instructed Rall to put up fortifications, assigning an engineering officer to assist in the task.[27] Rall chose to ignore these instructions. When his own second in command, Maj. Von Dechow, and other subordinates urged such precautions, he exclaimed, "Let them come! We want no trenches! We'll at them with the bayonet!"[28] He also proclaimed that he would soon be crossing the ice to advance on Philadelphia. Rall agreed only to outposts outside of town on the roads leading in. His contempt for the colonial army had begun influencing his judgment.

In spite of the secrecy used by Washington in his preparations, Rall began hearing rumors and reports of rebel activity several days before Christmas. Two deserters warned that militia were gathering in Pennsylvania and that several days' rations were being prepared.[29] On December 23 Dr. William Bryant, who lived near Trenton, sought out Col. Rall to tell him of a report from a Negro who had just crossed the river. He was informed that rebels were drawing rations and preparing to attack Trenton.[30] On Christmas Day an intelligence report was received from General James Grant at Princeton warning of an attack that day.[31] Although he continued to downplay these warnings, Rall ensured that one of his regiments was under arms and alert on Christmas Day.

During the day on December 25, Col. Rall went about his usual garrison routine. In the morning he inspected his men on parade and enjoyed the martial music played by his band.[32] After checking outposts around the outskirts of town in the afternoon, he returned to his quarters for a game of checkers with his host, Stacy Potts. At about 7:00 p.m. firing was heard on the north side of town as the Pennington Road outpost came under attack. The entire garrison in Trenton was immediately in an uproar. Reinforcements were dispatched to the outpost as Col. Rall assembled his regiment on the north side of town. Soon he began receiving reports. Six of his men had been wounded during an attack on the outpost by a force of about thirty colonial troops. After the rebels had broken off the attack, a patrol had gone up the Pennington Road about two miles but had found nothing. Maj. Von Dechow recommended a more extensive reconnaissance around Trenton.[33] Rall vetoed this proposal. It was his assumption that the rebel attack of which he had been forewarned had occurred. His contempt for the colonials only grew over this pitiful effort. He returned to Trenton to resume the Christmas revelry. What I call the Phantom Attack had taken place. The identity of the Americans who participated remains a mystery. Several sources contend that a patrol from a Virginia regiment made the probe of the Hessian outpost.[34] Another cited an advance party returning from New Jersey.[35] Others could only speculate that these were local farmers on a rampage over some grievance with the unpopular Hessians, or that they were a band of rebels.[36] The identity of those involved is less important than the critical nature of this incident, which was to prove decisive in the battle to follow. The timing and place of this "attack" and the resulting effect on Hessian preparedness can only be considered miraculous.

THE "UNOPENED NOTE"

Returning to town, Rall ordered a stand-down of his troops and allowed them to return to quarters in light of the miserable weather. He himself decided to join a Christmas party at Abraham Hunt's house, where he was able to play cards and drink into the night. Later in the evening a Tory farmer from Bucks County, Pennsylvania, knocked on the door and asked a servant to see Colonel Rall. The servant wouldn't let him in, telling him that the colonel was too busy to see anyone. The farmer wrote out a note explaining that the whole American army was crossing the river and marching on Trenton. His duty done, the farmer left and disappeared into the night. The servant delivered the note that Rall put into his pocket unread as he continued playing cards.[37] Unfortunately for him, he was not able to read the note written in English and felt no need to bother with a translation. The 'Unopened Note' was found the next day in the same pocket of a dying Colonel Rall. When informed of its contents he said, "If I had read this . . . I would not be here now."[38] If he had read the note events of the next day would have unfolded in a vastly different way.

THE BATTLE OF TRENTON

Totally unaware of these miraculous events working in his favor, Washington commenced his second crossing of the Delaware late on Christmas Day. To negotiate the ice-filled river, Washington again turned to Col. John Glover and his brigade of Massachusetts seamen. Using locally available 40-60 foot Durham boats, Glover's men ferried Washington's troops and artillery across the river starting just after darkness fell. A storm of wind, sleet, and snow raged throughout the night causing untold suffering among the ill-clad troops and Washington himself. The plan called for

The Attack on Trenton. (National Archives)

the crossing to be completed by midnight allowing for a five-hour march to Trenton and a predawn attack. The movement fell dangerously behind schedule due to the weather and state of the river. By 4 a.m., Washington's forces were finally advancing toward Trenton along two roads from the northeast.[39] Every man was half frozen, completely soaked, and certain that his musket would never fire. Even knowing the condition of his men and loss of darkness for cover, Washington pressed on. At about 7:45 a.m. the first outposts were encountered and quickly driven in. Surprise was complete as the Hessian units were caught in total confusion. Their officers assembled units piecemeal as small engagements were fought throughout the town. The American artillery, so laboriously brought across the river, proved decisive as it was brought into action at the head of the two main streets. Although musket fire was intermittent, cannon fire boomed down King and Queen streets breaking up attempted Hessian counterattacks.[40] Col. Rall himself tried to rally his men on the south side of town but was mortally wounded. By 9:00 a.m. Hessian units were surrendering or fleeing, and the battle was over.

In a few hours Washington had broken a Hessian brigade and had captured 900 prisoners and a stockpile of equipment, small arms, and artillery.[41] Several hundred escaped before the encirclement of the town was complete. The captives gazed in wonder at the bedraggled state of their conquerors. The Americans had lost two men frozen during the night and two officers and one man wounded. One of the wounded officers was Lieutenant James Monroe, destined to be a future president.[42] It had been in Washington's mind to continue on the offensive at this point. However, some of his units never made it across the river during the night. His men at Trenton were in no condition to do more. Washington marched his spent troops and captured Hessians back to McKonkey's Ferry to cross the Delaware again later on

The Hessians Surrender at Trenton. (National Archives)

the same day as the battle. There was no abatement of the fierce weather. Three more men froze to death in the boats. Washington found little time to speculate on what his army had accomplished.

THE AFTERMATH

In December 1776 the fire of American revolution was on the verge of being extinguished. New York and New Jersey were firmly in the hands of British and Tory forces. Philadelphia had been abandoned by the Congress and lay unprotected before the British advance. There was practically nothing left of the so-called Continental army, which was about to completely cease to exist with expiring enlistments. As far as the British and many Americans were concerned, the rebellion and so-called war were over.

The Battle of Trenton completely changed this picture. Among the troops immediately at hand Washington was able to get most to agree to continue their service. With new replacements arriving he was able to reoccupy Trenton on December 30 and to continue advancing on Princeton where another successful battle was fought on January 3, 1777. After this he moved to Morristown where he established a defensive enclave for the winter from which he could harass British supply lines through New Jersey. Washington's success emboldened local citizens to retaliate against the Hessian and British troops who had abused them during their months of occupation. British supply and troop movements were harassed everywhere. Howe was forced to abandon most of New Jersey back to New Brunswick and Perth Amboy where he could resupply by water from New York. Within these few days the war had taken on a completely new character.

News spread rapidly to the rest of the country. Confidence in George Washington and the Continental army took an upward turn. Suddenly it became less difficult to recruit new companies and regiments in every state. The commissary officers found it a little easier to collect food and supplies. People would at least consider taking Continental currency again. The Congress moved back to Philadelphia.[43]

When news of Trenton reached England, the reaction was shock and disillusionment. It was suddenly obvious that there would be no quick end to this war. Requests came in from Howe for twenty thousand more troops and for more ships to shore up an unsuccessful blockade. During the successes of the summer and fall, opposition to the war had fallen silent in Parliament. Whig supporters of the colonies began to once again find their voice. The aging William Pitt, now the Earl of Chatham, made a famous speech to the House of Lords warning of the possibility of France entering the war and reiterating the justness of the American cause. Pitt said, "We called them rebels, but they were only defending their unquestionable rights. Nor could we in any case conquer them—it was impossible." The resolve of the king and government did not disappear, although their problems in prosecuting a distant and increasingly unpopular war had suddenly escalated. Winston Churchill would comment about Trenton that "the effect of the stroke was out of all proportion to its military importance. It was the most critical moment in the war."[44]

The impact of Trenton was also felt in France. At first the French government had viewed the American revolution with uncertainty. There was considerable pleasure over England's difficulties and a constant search for opportunities to benefit from the conflict. However, there was a reluctance on the part of the king to openly support a rebellion against another crown. France also could not afford a direct military confrontation with England due to the weakness of her navy and vulnerability of her shipping. In early 1776 Silas Deane, a member of Congress, arrived in Paris to seek assistance for the American war effort. He got it in the form of a clandestine operation through a fictitious company called Hortalez et Cie.[45] Through this "company" quantities of clothing and ammunition were secretly forwarded to America and were extremely helpful to Washington during the early stages of the war. In December 1776 Benjamin Franklin arrived in Paris to join with Dean in seeking not only aid but also an alliance with France. This was not to happen for another year, but events at Trenton gave needed credibility to the diplomats' efforts.

BATTLE OF THE VIRGINIA CAPES 1781[46]

I have so far focused on a series of amazing incidents leading up to the even more amazing victory at Trenton. I have not at any point emphasized the decisions or the behavior of the leaders themselves, even though the actions of these leaders obviously had a large bearing on every outcome. I have avoided this area simply because it would be difficult to prove anything about God's influence in any particular decision or action. I believe that there have been times when God has inspired leaders to make good and even brilliant decisions, as well as times when he has allowed disastrous mistakes. An atheist might see nothing but a man succeeding due to his own ability or good fortune. However, this war does provide one instance where I believe God's hand can be seen in the decisions of George Washington and others, where the outcome is so improbable as to be considered miraculous. This instance involves the so-called Battle of the Virginia Capes, leading directly to the final confrontation at Yorktown.

By early 1781 the war with England dragged into its fifth year. The British were still fighting, and French aid had proven ineffective. A French naval squadron was blockaded in port at Newport, Rhode Island, leaving General Rochambeau's troops idle nearby. While the British continued a strong presence in New

York, General Cornwallis had captured Charleston in 1780, had decisively defeated Gates' army at Camden, and had advanced into North Carolina. George Washington, with the remnants of a 3,500-man army in New York, could do little to counter these moves. He continued to implore the Continental Congress for more support and the French for a greater naval presence. Keenly aware throughout the war of his vulnerability to British sea power, he had concluded that this aspect of the war was critical to the success of any strategy that he might devise.

It is difficult to appreciate command and control problems in an era of courier-delivered mail between units dispersed over thousands of miles. Plans and orders might be based on information weeks or months old and then be weeks or months in transit to the subordinate command concerned. Compared to the American/French problems in coordination, the British had the advantage of a fairly simple command structure. Washington had to rely on the uncertain support of his own political superiors and the cooperation of French army and naval commanders with unclear lines of authority. In dealing with all of these problems Washington had been extremely fortunate in being able to keep the war going for over four years while avoiding a catastrophic defeat. The task of focusing the required land and naval forces at a point to inflict a decisive defeat on his foe had proven impossible.

On August 14, 1781, Washington received information that seemed to offer an opportunity. A French frigate arrived in Newport with a dispatch from the French Admiral DeGrasse advising that he was departing the Caribbean with a fleet of twenty-five to thirty ships and embarked ground forces, heading for the Chesapeake Bay. At about the same time Washington received information from his forces in Virginia under Lafayette that Cornwallis was moving down the York peninsula toward Portsmouth. Although Washington did not know Cornwallis' intentions he felt that a long-awaited opportunity might be presenting itself. Reacting quickly, he put half of his army and all of Rochambeau's on the march toward Virginia, leaving the remainder of his forces to deceive the British in New York. Dispatches were sent to Lafayette to expect DeGrasse's force, and to deploy all available troops to prevent a British withdrawal. Orders were given to the French naval squadron in Newport, under Admiral DeBarras, to proceed to the Chesapeake.

Admiral DeGrasse reached the Chesapeake on August 30, debarking the troops that he brought and assisting the Americans in repositioning their forces. On September 5 a British fleet was sighted outside the entrance to the bay. Aware that DeBarras was coming from Newport and would be vulnerable to this new threat, DeGrasse gave up the safety of his position and sortied into the Atlantic. The Battle of the Virginia Capes ensued between the two fleets, both of which were roughly comparable in strength. After a sharp engagement late in the afternoon, action broke off at nightfall. Both sides had suffered significant damage and casualties although a decisive result was not achieved. For several days both fleets made repairs and maneuvered for position against each other. On the 9th, DeBarras finally arrived and slipped into the Chesapeake. With thirty-six French ships on the scene the British fleet withdrew, considering their chance gone to aid Cornwallis ashore or to inflict further damage on the French fleet. DeGrasse had masterfully accomplished his strategic mission and had given the American and French forces their first experience of naval superiority in any theater of the war. It was not to be wasted.

Over the next month the Revolutionary War reached its climax. Cornwallis went into a defensive position at Yorktown and for the first time experienced the frustration of being unable to resupply or reinforce, or even to withdraw, by sea. Washington had achieved a concentration of his own forces at the decisive moment, enabling a successful siege. On October 19 Cornwallis surrendered his entire army of 7,600 troops and what remained of British hopes for success in the war.

There were many good decisions made by Washington and DeGrasse leading to the favorable outcome at the Virginia Capes and, as a result, at Yorktown. Both commanders have justly been recognized for the brilliance of this campaign. Only when we consider the sequence of these events and the coordination of forces over vast distances do we see the miraculous nature of this victory and the hand of God at work. In *Sea Power* the authors state:

> Miracles do not often occur in military and naval operations, but Yorktown was a miracle. At a time when the American cause was disintegrating, it brought victory. At a time when the British could not effectively coordinate two armies in the colonies . . . it was an example of perfect coordination of a fleet with the armies of two different nations. At a time when communications were slow and unreliable, it demonstrated precise timing on the part of forces 1,500 miles apart.[47]

The co-author of *Sea Power* was Chester Nimitz, a prominent figure in World War II and Chapter Four of this book. As will be seen he was well acquainted with miraculous naval operations from firsthand experience.

GOD'S HAND IN THE REVOLUTIONARY WAR

In looking at any historical event it would be difficult to attribute a particular outcome to God's purpose. Especially in regard to a war, it would be largely futile to speculate on how God's purpose was served by the death of an individual, destruction of a unit, or

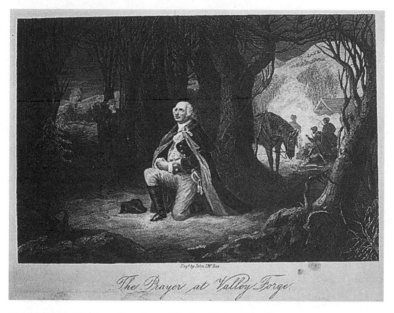

The Prayer at Valley Forge.

General Washington Praying. (National Archives)

outcome of a particular battle. It would even be difficult usually
to understand why one side ultimately prevailed over the other in
the war. At the time of the American Revolution, both England and
the colonies had similar cultures each with their share of political
leaders, soldiers, and citizens who were Christians. Prayers went
up from both sides of the Atlantic. Individuals and families suffered in both England and the colonies. It is not my belief that
God favored one side over the other. However, I do believe that
God had a purpose for this war and that his hand can be seen in
accomplishing it.

During the early stages of the developing conflict the individuals and groups involved in colonial resistance to the Crown
were very vulnerable and were proceeding cautiously. By early
1775 militia units were organizing in New England to resist

enforcement of the Intolerable Acts. The Continental Congress had drafted an appeal to King George. Sentiment favored reconciliation, as most were extremely apprehensive about the prospects of a war and the likely ruin to the colonies that would result. Many were dismayed when shots were fired at Lexington and Concord. It was a welcome relief that the colonial militia didn't fare too badly during these engagements. Even when forced off Breed's Hill the militia acquitted themselves well, to the surprise of the British regulars. By the time George Washington took command of the colonial units around Boston, a standoff had developed with the British garrison. During this tense period any forceful move by the British would have cut short this rebellion. Instead, these early challenges went largely unanswered. This "grace period" could be attributed to a lack of foresight on the part of General Gage or to confusion and inertia within the British government. The possibility should also be considered that this was part of the pattern of God's intervention in these events.

Washington's first offensive action in taking Dorchester Heights in early 1776 could also have had disastrous results. Howe had marshaled the troops to push Washington off the heights and had ordered the attack. Although British success was not a sure thing there would have been a bloody fight. If Howe had taken this position, it would not be difficult to envision a collapse of other parts of Washington's line around Boston. Again, the rebellion would have been over. To me, the fact that a violent storm came up at the right moment to make operations across Boston harbor impossible is further evidence that God's hand was at work. This storm was called a hurricane, although this was not hurricane season. These early successes led directly to the vote for independence within the Congress on July 4. This historic event would not have been possible without an apparently successful army in the field. If Washington's troops had been routed or even soundly defeated, it is hard to believe that the Congress would have cast such a vote or even have remained much longer in existence.

In the summer of 1776 General Howe arrived in New York with an army of overwhelming strength to finally put an end to the colonial uprising. After unwisely committing himself to defending Long Island, Washington found his forward positions turned and routed. As he desperately tried to reorganize on Brooklyn Heights, General Howe saw an opportunity to bring his fleet behind Washington to cut him off and bring his force under naval gunfire. Again, nature cooperated as strong northeast winds kept the British fleet from advancing up the East River during the time when this could have been disastrous for the colonials. On August 29 Washington decided that he had to take his army off Long Island and found conditions perfect on the same East River for a night withdrawal by boat. As troops selectively abandoned the lines within musket range of the British any alarm would have spelled disaster. The boatlift went on uninterrupted throughout a long night. I believe that we can see further evidence of God's hand at work during this tense night and again the next morning when an unexpected fog appeared over the river to mask the last few hours of the evacuation. Setting a pattern for much of the war, Washington, with God's help, achieved a victory by surviving. Howe lost another opportunity to end the rebellion.

Events leading up to the Battle of Trenton continued to show the hand of God at work in carrying the young nation through its darkest hours. The unusual move by Charles Lee to spend a night away from his command and his strange capture by British dragoons finally resulted in Washington receiving the troops that he needed to consider offensive action. The "Phantom Attack" and the "Unread Note" each played a key part in the amazing victory at Trenton. Without these miraculous events, Washington would have encountered an alert and ready Hessian brigade. As was the case during the entire war, a defeat of his army could have ended the war for Washington and America. On the other hand, without this victory the Continental army would have dissolved for other reasons, exposing Philadelphia to immediate capture and an equally certain end to the war.

In December 1776, after the Battle of Trenton, it was not obvious to George Washington or anyone else that a major turning point in the Revolutionary War had been reached. Washington was still pleading with Congress for more troops and supplies and with his own men to extend their enlistments. There were years of hard campaigning ahead with a never-ending struggle just to keep an army in the field. Fighting would range over the continent from Canada to Georgia and onto the oceans. The Continental army would fight on doggedly to keep the revolution alive. Washington would never have the luxury of feeling like he was in control of the war. Most often his only victories would have to be found in avoiding catastrophic defeat. At Trenton, Washington overtly risked such a defeat. Without the "Phantom Attack" and the "Unopened Note," he would have marched the remnants of his army into a disaster. Instead, with God's help, he achieved a resounding triumph, against staggering odds. This astonishing victory came at the most crucial moment, the last hour, saving the struggling revolution. By this victory God ensured that the war would go on. Never again would the new nation be so close to extinction. Washington would get wiser in conserving his forces. France would eventually make her military presence felt. Finally, at the Virginia Capes and Yorktown a miracle of timing and coordination would occur giving Washington the final victory.

GOD'S PURPOSE IN THE CAUSE OF FREEDOM

The American Revolution clearly has a unique place in human history. Over more than a century the Old World had planted and nourished the seed of a New World in North America. The various English colonies that developed during this time were extremely diverse with a multitude of different cultures and economic systems. They also had some unusual things in common. The people that left Europe generally had less of a stake in the Old World structures that they left behind. They were more adventurous, individualistic, and less subordinated to authority. Religion was important to these people, but more on an individual basis, with less attachment to official church structures and prescribed practices. I believe that during the 1600s and into the next century God was creating a situation in the New World where a new beginning was possible for man's political and religious institutions. An opportunity was being presented to achieve a level of human freedom unique so far in modern history.

I believe that in the 1700s God was ready for this new beginning to flourish in America. However, it was not going to be easy. Most people then as now were satisfied with the status quo and afraid of change. After the French and Indian War most colonialists were happier than ever to be under British protection, and an underlying loyalty to the British crown was deeply ingrained. It took more than a decade of Parliament mismanagement and royal indifference to stir the seeds of discontent into a rebellion. On the American side it took a hard core of dissidents ready to create an uproar over any perceived infringement of rights by England. Many of the taxes imposed during this period were equitable in themselves, and colonial resistance was often unreasonable. English reaction to this resistance only spread discontent over a wider area of the population. Although many worked to diffuse the growing tension, the conflict was serving to bring together the diverse and highly individualistic societies making up the English colonies into a common American cause. The cause was freedom, in accordance with God's purpose.

Some religious historians feel that an integral part of the movement toward revolution was the phenomenon of spiritual revival during the 1730s and '40s known generally as the Great Awakening.[48] This occurrence was actually a series of widely separated episodes of spiritual renewal. Within the Dutch Reformed Church in New Jersey, Theodore Freylinghuysen began preaching a message of individual salvation transcending church orthodoxy. Gilbert Tennant was also preaching a message of personal salvation within the Presbyterian Church emphasizing that pleasing God involved more than the formalities of church membership. In New England Jonathan Edwards led a revival with similar themes. All of these separate movements took on a larger focus with the arrival of George Whitfield from England in 1738.[49] Whitfield was an Anglican priest and an unforgettable preacher who was moved to take his message outside the formal church into public and even open-air settings. On his mission he journeyed across the Atlantic thirteen times preaching the message of personal salvation up and down the East Coast. The efforts of these evangelists led other itinerant preachers to travel throughout the colonies preaching that salvation was to be found in individual repentance and a personal relationship with God. The message was clear that God does not work through kings, bishops, and the upper classes, but among the people themselves. The message fell on receptive ears as crowds flocked to these preachers.[50]

These itinerant preachers of the Awakening carried no sanction of church authority. All that they had was the spiritual

authority of the Bible and their own persuasiveness. They recognized that no act of repentance was meaningful without the
complete free will of the individual. In many cases the structured
authority and worship of the established churches worked against
recognition of this truth, especially in England with its long history of interrelated church and government. I believe that this
concept of free will is completely in accordance with God's plan
for his creation. He does not intend to compel us to seek him. I
believe that he is not pleased when some attempt to force others
toward him through institutional, political, or religious pressure.
The Awakening seemed to draw large numbers of people throughout the colonies back toward a more direct relationship to God
based on their willing and personal acceptance of his salvation.[51]
This widespread phenomenon had a definite effect on the political
climate during the 1760s and '70s as more and more people in the
colonies found themselves questioning and challenging the crown
of England and established political authority. I believe that it was
God's will that a new political system came into being based on
personal and religious freedom, to establish a new climate of free
will for men to chose their own spiritual direction.

The Lord says: You have not obeyed me; you have not
proclaimed freedom for your fellow countrymen.
So I now proclaim 'freedom' for you—'freedom' to
fall by the sword.

—JEREMIAH 34:17

CHAPTER THREE

THE CIVIL WAR— MOMENT OF DECISION

A FTER INFLICTING *a series of defeats on each Union army sent against him, Robert E. Lee invaded Maryland in early September 1862. Daringly, he divided his forces, counting on the cautious and deliberate nature of the newly assigned George B. McClellan to give him time to accomplish several objectives. In Washington, the Lincoln administration was under increasing attack for mishandling the war. Under stress, Lincoln had decided to issue a proclamation freeing the slaves in the rebellious states, but was afraid to proceed in the face of recurring military disasters. In England it appeared that the war might actually be ending as the prime minister and cabinet prepared to broker a peace settlement and even to recognize the Confederacy. On September 13 all was going according to Lee's plan. Harpers Ferry was under siege and his advance units were approaching Hagerstown. Union communications to the west were cut and McClellan's army was being drawn away from its bases, with lengthening supply lines and growing uncertainty. A few more days would give Lee the opportunity to consolidate his forces at a time and place of his choosing and to fight the decisive battle that would probably end the war. Lee's inexorable march toward victory was interrupted, however, by one of the unluckiest incidents in history. At the moment of climax, the fate of the nation would again be in the hand of God.*

RELIGION AFTER THE REVOLUTION

During the early 1800s religious life in the young United States continued to be diverse and energetic. All congregations experienced growth and flourished with recurring revival energy. Even the Anglicans began to recover from their identification with Toryism as the Protestant Episcopal Church was organized.[52] Early efforts to establish churches in certain areas were finally discontinued as the separation of church and state became accepted. Churches in America would truly be built on the power of the gospel and the evangelical efforts of clergy and laypeople. Much energy of every church was soon focused on the westward expansion of the nation and the need to carry Christianity into the frontier. This righteous fervor to extend the faith was the original basis of the concept of manifest destiny, which the less scrupulous would use to justify the inexorable incorporation of western territories into the nation.[53] There was also an awakening among many religious people to the moral dilemma posed by slavery. To many, the promise of the Declaration of Independence was unfulfilled and would continue to be until every person in the nation was free. At first this was a question of conscience, and men of conscience in the North and South freely raised and debated the issue. Gradually, it became an economic and political issue at the center of a national fracture and catastrophic war.

Author's Note: At this point I feel the need to assert my standing as a Southerner. I come from many generations of South Carolinians and strongly consider myself to be of the Old South. I know that many of similar background will disagree with the emphasis that I place on slavery in this narrative. My own mother taught me that the divisive issues of the time were industrial and agricultural policy, tariffs, and states' rights. I don't wish to minimize these issues, as I have always considered them valid. I believe that what most troubles Southerners in regard to slavery as a "cause" of the Civil War is the assumption that the Union side was pursuing some higher moral cause. I will to a considerable extent dispel that notion by showing the human failures of all parties to the conflict and how, I believe, God worked in these events to accomplish his own purpose.

POLITICAL ISSUES

In 1860 the Republican candidate, Abraham Lincoln, was elected president of the United States with a little over one-third of the popular vote and 180 of 303 electoral votes. The Democratic Party was hopelessly divided between Southern and Northern wings, with each fielding its own presidential ticket, ensuring the party's defeat at the polls. Southern leaders had vowed to secede from the Union if the Republican Party, with its anti-Southern bias, was victorious at the polls. On December 20, 1860, South Carolina passed an ordinance of secession and was soon followed by six other Southern states. The new narrowly elected president faced an immense crisis with a shaky political base. To many, using force to prevent secession was unthinkable. Lincoln took the stand that the Union had to be preserved. In his inaugural address he argued that if minorities were allowed to secede over grievances, there would be no end to further subdivision and anarchy. He asserted that the Constitution could not be "peaceably unmade by less than all the parties who made it."[54] Many would contest this stand, instead advocating that the Southern states be allowed to go their own way. Even many abolitionists considered secession an answer to their moral objections over slavery.[55] The Southern leaders had staked everything on the belief that this view would prevail, with or without armed conflict.[56]

There were many political, economic, and cultural issues causing trouble between North and South. However, the one irreconcilable issue at the center of the political crisis was the institution of slavery. Slavery had always been a key ingredient in the cotton economy and culture of the South. At one time thought to be on the decline, it had undergone a resurgence with development of the cotton gin, industrialization of the spinning and weaving processes, and a booming cotton trade. Between 1845 and the early 1850s the price of cotton had more than doubled, making cotton more of a viable crop than ever, so long as slavery was an integral part of the production process.[57] In the Northern states where it had been abolished, slavery was seen by many as a fundamental contradiction to the principles articulated in the Declaration of Independence. To some the issue of freedom transcended economics and property rights. Many others may have agreed intellectually but were content with the status quo based on Southern prosperity. Over the years the political process had strained to resolve these disparate views. The Democratic Party had remained in power in Washington by compromising between regional factions. Unfortunately, consensus evaporated during the 1860 Convention with a walkout of Southern delegates and a fractured party.

Lincoln and the Republican Party came to power with a clear antipathy toward slavery. Lincoln's frequently expressed view was that slavery was morally wrong and should eventually be eliminated, even though he had no apparent timetable for this process or clear idea of how it would be accomplished. The Republicans' one clear position was that slavery should not be allowed to expand.[58] This issue of extending slavery into the western territories had been the flash point of the slavery dispute for decades. Even so, except for a small vocal minority, there had never been any serious political move to abolish slavery where it was already in place. It was well established under the Constitution that the federal government had no right to interfere with slavery in the states. No one had a solution to the problem of compensating slave owners for their property or of what would become of millions of slaves if freed. Prejudice and fear of Negroes not under the complete control of slave laws was common in all regions of the country. Also merchants and manufacturers throughout the North were prospering from sales to the Southern cotton economy. If slavery was a cancer, apparently it was one that couldn't be removed without killing the patient. As the states of the Deep South began seceding in late 1860 Lincoln repeatedly reassured the South that slavery in their states was not in jeopardy. His concern was for the Union. In his first inaugural address he repeated his own quoted remark that, "I have no purpose, directly or indirectly, to interfere with the institution of slavery in the States where it exists." He even agreed to support a constitutional amendment guaranteeing slavery in the slave states.[59]

EMANCIPATION

As armed conflict began in 1861 Lincoln clung to the hope that the Union could be restored to its former state. He continued to believe that slave rights had to be guaranteed to encourage the efforts of Unionists in the South and to maintain the loyalty of the border states. Agitation continued within his cabinet,

Congress, and elements of the public for outright freeing of the slaves. Lincoln resisted. When one of his generals refused to hand back fugitive slaves fleeing into Union lines Lincoln objected, fearing border state reaction.[60]

As time passed and the fighting grew more bitter, his view on slavery began to change slowly. Some tried to convince him of the absurdity of fighting a war without attacking a root cause of it. He was told that Great Britain might be discouraged in its support of the South if abolishment of slavery were to become an aim of the war.[61] In 1861 Lincoln began to consider a plan to gradually eliminate slavery in the border states with federal compensation and colonization outside the country. Once the rebellion was put down, the same plan could be implemented in the South. He presented these ideas in his annual message to Congress in December 1861.[62]

Meanwhile, the war was going badly for the North. Lincoln's generals would not fight and when they did, the results were usually not encouraging. Casualties mounted. Public dissatisfaction grew. Lincoln's own attitude toward the South hardened. Even the border states opposed his proposals for gradual abolishment of slavery with compensation. He came to see the futility of upholding Constitutional protections for those in rebellion against the Constitution. In July 1862 he told senators and representatives of the vorder states that restoration of the Union with slavery was no longer possible.[63] On July 21 he informed his cabinet that he was ready to take executive action to emancipate slaves in the rebel states. Some cheered. Some were astonished. His secretary of state and trusted advisor, William H. Seward, agreed with the idea but was vehemently opposed to the timing. Since the Union had won no victories in the field, he declared that such a proclamation would appear to be a "despairing cry—a shriek from the Administration."[64] Lincoln listened and had to agree. He couldn't allow this proclamation to appear to be a measure of desperation.

Union Infantry on Parade. (National Archives)

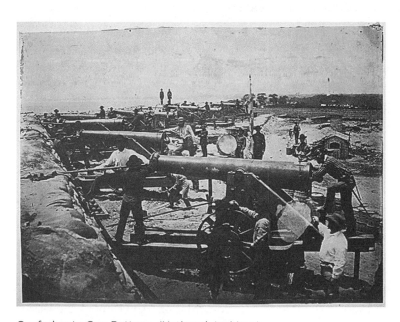

Confederate Gun Battery. (National Archives)

He needed a military victory. The Emancipation Proclamation went into his desk drawer.

DIPLOMACY

On May 14, 1861, Queen Victoria proclaimed British neutrality in the developing war and conferred belligerent status upon the Confederacy, in effect acknowledging it as a responsible government engaged in war. Secretary of State Seward was incensed that Britain had thus rejected the Union interpretation of the war as a domestic insurrection. He feared that Britain was moving toward full recognition of the Confederacy as a nation. If this were to happen, France and other European nations would undoubtedly do the same. Such recognition would probably spell the end of the North's hope to prevail in the conflict. In this situation Lincoln permitted a hard line, as recommended by Seward, threatening war if Britain recognized the South.[65]

Seward's hard line seemed to work, although relations with Britain were to continue strained. There was in fact considerable support for the South in England. Why shouldn't the Southern states get their independence as the thirteen colonies had? Monarchists throughout Europe were encouraged by the apparent inability of the new democratic government to perpetuate itself. Also, Lincoln continued to insist that repeal of slavery was not a goal of the war. Therefore, the war was in fact a dispute over interpretation of the American constitution. There was also concern over continuing hostilities and disruption of the cotton trade, with possible idling of factories in England.[66]

British sentiment was further tilted toward the Confederacy due to the so-called Trent Affair. In November 1861 a federal warship intercepted the British ship *Trent* off the coast of Cuba and took two Confederate commissioners prisoner. The British were enraged and at once began preparing for war. The immediate crisis was eased only when Lincoln gave assurances that the Union captain acted without authority and further agreed to release the commissioners. Union enforcement of its blockade would be a source of continuing tension with Britain.[67]

As the war continued in 1862 the European powers waited. On the battlefield the Confederacy was proving its viability. After Lee's success in defending Richmond in June and July, intense debate ensued in Britain over the question of intervention and mediation of the conflict. After the Union disaster at the Second Battle of Manassas on July 29 it actually appeared that the war might be ending. In early August the prime minister initiated

President
Abraham
Lincoln.
(National
Archives)

discreet plans for an armistice proposal. A cabinet meeting was planned for late October to consider a brokered peace based on separation. If this were to fail there was sentiment to proceed with full recognition of the Confederacy.[68]

MILITARY OPERATIONS

Early in the war, theaters of operation developed in the East and West. Union efforts in the West were designed to save Kentucky, take the Mississippi, and split the Confederacy. These aims were strategically important. However, center stage was in the East where Union and Confederate capitols lay separated by less than one hundred miles of rolling Virginia countryside. For over a year the citizens of Washington lived under dire fear of imminent destruction. Richmond would face the same anxiety later. All the world's attention was focused on this small area and the most costly, intense fighting in history.

After the first Union disaster at Manassas Junction in July 1861, Lincoln turned to the thirty-five-year-old George B. McClellan. With an exemplary military record the young general took command of the Army of the Potomac with great energy and fanfare. With public expectation for victory running high, quick results were anxiously awaited. Instead McClellan went into a protracted period of reorganization and retraining stretching over the fall and winter months of 1861–62. As Lincoln urged action, McClellan became increasingly irritated and remote. At every step politicians were looking over his shoulder. At one point Lincoln sarcastically remarked that, if McClellan didn't want to use the Army of the Potomac, he would like to borrow it.[69]

In March 1862 McClellan was finally ready to resume the fighting in a controversial move by water to the peninsula between the James and York rivers to attack Richmond from the East. Lincoln was never comfortable with this strategy although he was reluctant to interfere with his new commander in chief.[70] After an unnecessary month-long siege of Yorktown, McClellan achieved several successes at Williamsburg and Fair Oaks in May. Unfortunately for McClellan, the Confederate commander, Joseph E. Johnston, was wounded at Fair Oaks, and Robert E. Lee took command of the Southern forces. Lee quickly took the offensive and in what are now known as the Seven Days Battles, between June 25 and July 1, fought McClellan back to Harrison's Landing on the James River. This in effect lifted the siege of Richmond. Southern morale soared as the North's hopes for a quick end to the war were extinguished.

Having achieved some success commanding Union forces in the West, Gen. John Pope was placed in command of the newly constituted Army of Virginia in June 1862. As McClellan's offensive on the peninsula came to a halt, Pope opened another front by maneuvering his army toward Richmond from the North generally along the line of the Orange and Alexandria railroad. Leaving minimal forces to hold McClellan, Lee further divided his forces to outmaneuver and confound Pope. By August 31, the Second Battle of Manassas concluded with a decisive rout of Pope's army. Once again crisis filled the air in Washington. Lincoln's problems mounted as he reached one of the low points of his life. Alone at his desk, he wrote, "The will of God prevails. In the present civil war it is quite possible that God's purpose is something different from the purpose of either party—God wills this contest, and wills that it shall not end yet. He could give the final victory to either side any day. Yet the contest proceeds."[71]

On September 5 Lee invaded Maryland. With no other seasoned commanders at hand, Lincoln again turned to McClellan to take the field and meet the invasion. He actually had no other choice at that point, although his critics derided his decision. Events seemed to be moving to some great climax. As McClellan

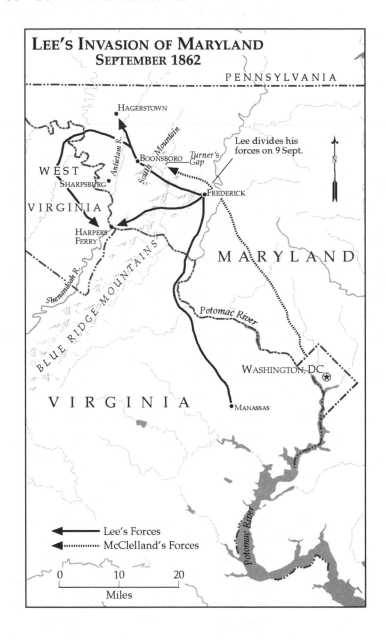

departed with his army, Lincoln made a covenant with himself and God."[72] If a victory were won, he would take this as "an indication of Divine Will that it was his duty to move forward in the work of emancipation." The Emancipation Proclamation waited.

LEE'S OFFENSIVE

By early September Robert E. Lee's victorious army was ragged and weary. It was Lee's genius, however, not to surrender the initiative. His own fighting spirit uplifted his troops to further and even greater effort. Sensing the futility of a direct assault on Washington, Lee planned a campaign into Western Maryland and Pennsylvania that would draw McClellan ever further away from his base and leave either his army or the capitol vulnerable.[74] First, Lee moved his army from Northern Virginia, across the Potomac, and to Frederick, Maryland. He then turned west through South Mountain, a long spur of the Blue Ridge running north from the Potomac River into Western Maryland. Leaving General Stuart's cavalry east of the mountain to screen his movements, Lee again divided his army. Jackson went south to take the Union stronghold at Harpers Ferry. Longstreet moved north toward Hagerstown. Gen. D. H. Hill moved to Boonesboro with the mission of defending Turner's Gap and keeping McClellan from crossing South Mountain. Lee was relying on McClellan's cautious nature to allow time to complete these maneuvers and to reassemble the Confederate forces around Hagerstown for a decisive engagement at a time and place of Lee's own choosing.

MOMENT OF DECISION—THE LOST ORDER

At this moment a seemingly small incident occurred which altered the course of Lee's campaign and the war. The movements of Lee's

General Robert E. Lee. (National Archives)

army were outlined in Headquarters Army of Northern Virginia Special Order Number 191 dated September 9, 1862, and signed by Col. R. H. Chilton, Lee's adjutant-general. Copies of this order were disseminated on that date to Lee's division commanders, including D. H. Hill, then located near Frederick.[75] Shortly all Confederate units were on the move. By late morning on September 13th Union troops of the 27th Indiana Volunteers of the Twelfth Army Corps arrived in Frederick and stacked arms on the same ground occupied previously by D. H. Hill's division. Shortly after stacking their weapons, several soldiers, including Sergeant John Bloss and Corporal B. W. Mitchell, found three cigars on the ground wrapped in a piece of paper. Upon examination, the piece of paper looked official.[76] Sergeant Bloss immediately went to Regimental Headquarters. The order was quickly forwarded to Division Headquarters, where Captain Samuel E. Pittman, the acting division adjutant-general, examined it. It so happened that Pittman had known Col. Chilton before the war and was able to verify Chilton's signature and thus the authenticity of the order. Pittman had been a bank teller in Detroit where Chilton had been the paymaster for a nearby army unit. He had cashed checks for Chilton on many occasions. Without that small "coincidence," the piece of paper found on the field might have been considered a fake or even an attempted deception on the part of the Confederates.

Within hours, Special Order No. 191 was in the hands of George B. McClellan. For the first time the veil was lifted for the Union commander. He could at last see where his opponent was and what he was doing. A few days before he had written to Gen. Halleck: "Our information is still entirely too indefinite to justify definite action."[77] On the 13th he wrote the president, "I have all the plans of the Rebels . . . Lee has made a gross mistake and . . . he will be severely punished for it."[78] Realizing that Lee's army was scattered and that he was positioned to divide and conquer, McClellan put his army on the march.

Momentous events unfolded within the next few days. Even with his advantage, McClellan lost precious time in forcing his way through the passes and saw a golden opportunity slip away. Even so, Lee had to focus all his energies to reassemble his scattered divisions. He called for all units to gather at the little town of Sharpsburg, where he hastily occupied positions on the high ground overlooking Antietam Creek. On September 15 he had about 18,000 troops on the scene. McClellan deliberately made his preparations. By the 16th Jackson arrived from Harpers Ferry, doubling the Southern force, but still facing McClellan's army of 87,000. Finally, at dawn on the next day, Gen. Joseph Hooker's I Corps launched the Union assault on Lee's left flank, leading to a day-long battle of fierce intensity. Within twelve hours there were 25,000 casualties, one of the bloodiest struggles in history. Lee's army was practically decimated but held on. McClellan was incredibly close to destroying his opponent, but he didn't seem to know it. Both armies faced each other the next day without action. Finally, on the night of the 18th Lee pulled back, recrossing the Potomac. Tactically, the Battle of Antietam was a standoff. Strategically, the invasion was turned back. Lee himself concluded that the 'Lost Order' was a major reason for the failure of his Maryland campaign.[79] Due entirely to that small incident, he had been forced to fight at a time and place not of his choosing, with many of his units arriving piecemeal on the battlefield. For once he could not accomplish the impossible. The high tide of the Confederacy had been reached.

THE AFTERMATH

In September 1862 it would have been difficult to detect a major turning point in the war favorable to the North. McClellan totally failed to follow up his advantage and allowed Lee to retire in an orderly fashion with his depleted army basically intact. Lincoln was furious. By November he would fire McClellan for good.[80] For another year Lee would go on inflicting stunning defeats on his new adversaries and would again invade Maryland in 1863, culminating in the Battle of Gettysburg. A lot of blood would yet be shed on the battlefield.

General George B. McClellan. (National Archives)

The decisive and lasting impact of the reversal at Antietam can be seen on the political and diplomatic fronts.[81] As shown, Lincoln was waiting for an opportunity to act on his proclamation freeing the slaves. Whether he took the results at Antietam to be an answer to his prayer and to his promise to God or whether this was a calculated political move on his part is largely irrelevant. The time had come to act. On September 22 he assembled his cabinet to read and discuss his draft proclamation. He announced his intention to free slaves in the rebellious states and to ask Congress for gradual emancipation in the loyal states accompanied by a colonization program. Support was not unanimous. There was still concern for reaction in the border states. Lincoln did not entertain objections. He could no longer allow the border states to dictate. The war had finally gone too far and become too terrible. He had finally crossed the line. On September 23, 1862, Lincoln issued the Emancipation Proclamation, ordering that on January 1, 1863, "all persons held as slaves within any state . . . then in rebellion against the United States shall be then, thenceforward, and forever free."[82]

The immediate reaction to Lincoln's proclamation was not all encouraging. Negative sentiment was heard from the border states and from Democrats, threatening the president's tenuous war coalition. The fall elections went badly for the Republicans and saw them lose their majorities in the five most populous Northern states, while barely retaining control of Congress. War weariness contributed in some degree to these unfavorable election results. On the positive side, the Republicans, the abolitionists, and large numbers of ordinary citizens were uplifted and energized. For some the root cause of the war was being addressed and a moral dimension added. The war would no longer be fought for only an abstract constitutional principle. Human freedom was now at stake.

Reaction in England was also mixed. Much of the press and many politicians thought the proclamation absurd since it abolished slavery only in those areas where the federal government was powerless to act. Some editorial opinion was positive and there was considerable popular reaction among working-class people, with demonstrations in London, Birmingham, and other cities. The reaction that counted, however, was within the British cabinet. The Emancipation Proclamation, combined with news about Lee's retreat into Virginia after Antietam, caused the cabinet to indefinitely postpone further consideration of intervention in the American war or of recognition of the Confederacy. Even though support for the South would continue widespread, there could be no question of England taking an official position that could be viewed as supporting slavery or opposing freedom.[83] Even the cotton trade couldn't compete with the power of this idea.

GOD'S HAND

In his second inaugural address, a few weeks before his assassination, President Lincoln expressed his own doubts about how God might view this war: "Both (sides) read the same Bible, and pray to the same God; and each invokes his aid against the other ... The prayers of both could not be answered. That of neither has been answered fully. The Almighty has His own purposes."[84] He was articulating the difficulty in discerning God's purpose in a battle or in a war—especially one of citizen against citizen, of brother against brother. As I have already explained, I address this same question with great humility. What was God's purpose in the Civil War? It is my belief that in looking back we can see God's will at work in the 1800s to abolish slavery in the United States of America. If this belief is in fact true, many events associated with that war do truly seem inevitable, in retrospect, and shaped by divine will.

By 1860 slavery was a firmly established institution in large regions of the United States. For decades the political power of the Southern states had been strong in Congress. The Democratic Party maintained its control of the White House by consistently supporting Southern interests and protecting slavery. The electorate in the North was generally content with the status quo.

Slavery was the direct basis of the Southern economy and to a large extent of the Northern economy as well. Northern manufacturers and merchants were happy with the goods and services being purchased by a prosperous South. Few were willing to consider the question of how to cope with millions of Negroes not under strict control. In 1857 the Supreme Court handed down the Dred Scott decision, reaffirming the primacy of property rights under the Constitution as pertaining to slavery. By the time of the 1860 election, political debate raged over extending slavery into the western territories, but not over slavery as it then existed anywhere. Even the Republican Party didn't challenge slavery in the South, and, even as the Southern states were seceding, Lincoln offered to support a Constitutional amendment guaranteeing the existence of slavery in the South. Slavery was not going away by means of any normal political process.

Was war then the only answer? Could this war have been in accordance with God's plan? It is difficult to believe that any war could be in God's plan. However, by 1860 there didn't seem to be any other way. Looking back further in time there may have been other possibilities. For a period of time in the early 1800s the antislavery movement had a more conciliatory tone. Led by Christian clergy, there was a belief that the Christian approach of appealing to the conscience of slave owners would eventually be successful. Many in the South had doubts of their own about slavery. Robert E. Lee wrote in 1856 that "slavery as an institution is a moral and political evil."[85] Jefferson Davis, the president of the Confederate States, was himself a slaveholder. In an 1848 speech he had stated that he did not consider slavery in the United States to be a permanent condition, although it might take several generations to prepare the slaves to live as free men.[86] If only he and other national leaders had seriously considered ways to do this. Perhaps there was a time when men of good will from all areas of the country could have discussed ways to phase out slavery and to incorporate the freed slaves into the national economy. Unfortunately, however, the full spectrum of human weakness gradually prevailed. The problem was too difficult to figure out. Slavery was too integral to the Southern culture and national economy. Prejudice against the Negro was too ingrained. The abolitionist attacks disregarded all practical problems, wounded Southern pride, and stiffened resistance. Public doubt became impossible and finally disappeared in the South. Even the clergy in the South eventually found themselves presenting biblical arguments for slavery. Mankind had devised slavery over many centuries. Unfortunately, mankind was unable to solve the riddle of its unmaking. Apparently it was God's plan that it finally come to an end. Only cataclysmic events would make it happen.

In assessing the relative strengths of the North and South in manpower and resources, it was inevitable that the North would prevail in a long war. The South's population of 9 million, including over 3 million slaves was far short of the North's 23 million.[87] Looking at the balance of power, there is in fact no reason why the war should not have been over in a few months, just as Lincoln hoped would be the case. In the beginning both armies were hastily assembled and put into the field. The South seemed to be more effective in its early efforts at mobilization. A more vigorous effort by the North and a bolder Union commander should have accomplished an early invasion of Virginia and capture of Richmond. The war would have been over. However, if this had happened, the status quo would have remained. The issue of secession would have been settled, but the issue of slavery would have remained as before. Cautious Union commanders and the bold genius of Robert E. Lee ensured that the war would go on. In fact Lee took the South to the verge of outright victory during the summer of 1862. The Northern populace tasted the bitter frustration of military defeat and growing casualties. The "Lost Order" and the resulting Battle of Antietam finally interrupted Lee's march toward ultimate victory. With this reversal the political and diplomatic picture changed and the ultimate military result became inevitable. The material might of the North would increasingly be brought to bear.

It is my belief that the war had to reach this peak in 1862 to finally doom slavery. The war had gone on for over a year and Lincoln continued to cling to his position of preserving slavery in the border and even rebelling states, always hoping to return the nation to its former status. Union victory or a negotiated peace in 1861 or 1862 would have left slavery intact. Lincoln's proclamation of September 23 in fact left the door open until January 1, 1863. If a state in rebellion were to return to the Union by that date, the proclamation would not apply there. Lincoln hoped that this would actually happen. However, not only did no Confederate states renounce the rebellion, a significant Southern victory was achieved at Fredericksburg in December 1862. The January 1st deadline passed with no end to the war in sight and with only escalating horror on the battlefield. The final line had been crossed. Prophetically, Lee had written, "How long their (the Negroes) subjugation may be necessary is known and ordered by a wise and merciful Providence."[88] By eerie coincidence, whether in reality or in delusion, Lincoln in 1862 had begun to see himself as an " instrument of Providence," placed at the center of the war for God's own designs.[89] Events seemed to be moving out of the hands of soldiers and politicians. God's hand had taken control. The South would not succeed. Slavery was finally doomed. The tragedy would now go on to its final, inevitable conclusion.

Throughout this period men struggled on the battlefield and in the political arena. There were great men and small men. Each lived his own life and made his own contribution to events of the time. Issues were complex and the struggles difficult. There were many men seeking to do God's will and many seeking God's justification for their own will. It's not easy to look back and to see what God's will was in every situation, just as it isn't easy today. For any individual to truly hear God, I believe he has to earnestly try to walk with God and to do a lot of listening. There has to be surrender to the fact that God is in control. He has a design. We do the right thing when we align ourselves with his plans. It is never easy. I certainly don't think that it was easy for any individual living during the Civil War. In retrospect, God's purpose in eliminating slavery may seem clear to me now. It may have been clear to a few abolitionists at the time. To most, however, God's will was not clear or was not even considered. Most probably hoped and prayed God was on their side, yet God worked out his own purpose in his own way. He shaped men and events, often in ways unknown to them. I believe that we can clearly see his hand at work in the case of the 'Lost Order' and all of the events surrounding this incident. Was George B. McClellan lucky? Was Robert E. Lee unlucky? I am sure that both had their own answers to those questions. It is my belief that there was much more to this story than luck. This incident was one piece of the pattern of events that finally came together to extend the promise of the Declaration of Independence and American Revolution to every citizen of the United States.

Call upon me in the day of trouble; I will deliver you.

—PSALM 50:15

CHAPTER FOUR

WORLD WAR II— THE TIDE TURNS

O N MAY 28, 1942, *the most powerful fleet ever seen up to that time set course for Midway Island in the center of the Pacific Ocean. The Japanese Navy was committed to finishing the job started at Pearl Harbor six months before. The small American carrier fleet had been untouched in that attack due to bad timing, and these three ships were proving to be an unexpected annoyance. At this time the Japanese military machine had not been stopped anywhere during over ten years of conquest in China, Southeast Asia, and the Pacific, and allied resistance continued to crumble on all fronts. The Battle of Midway was to be the climactic victory for the Japanese, eliminating American power in the Pacific for the foreseeable future and even leaving the U.S. West Coast without protection. Over two hundred ships were committed to ensure success, including eleven battleships and eight aircraft carriers. By every calculation of the odds, this victory was as close to a sure thing as it is possible to achieve in war. However, on June 4, as the opposing fleets came to grips, a series of apparently random events began to unfold which changed those odds. God's hand seemed to take control at the crucial moment of World War II.*

EARLY JAPAN

Japan has always been something of a mystery to Americans. For most of her history before World War II this was no accident. Japan has had a unique history of isolation. Its four main islands are separated from the Asian mainland by the Sea of Japan and from one to five hundred miles of open water. From end to end the island chain is about the length of the East Coast of the United States, but in land area is about the size of Montana. The islands are mostly mountainous, with only about 15 percent of the land farmable. The populated areas are mostly found close to the coast. Originally, Mongolians came from Asia via the Korean peninsula to settle the islands. In their isolation, the Japanese people have since existed as one of the most homogeneous populations in the world. An enduring feature of the economy has been the cultivation of rice on small plots with shared labor and community irrigation systems. All aspects of Japan's geography and economic development worked to shape a culture uniquely focused within and centered on values of cooperation and common effort. These values have been reinforced at times by political decree.

RELIGION

The religious history of Japan has been rich and complex. Its earliest roots are found in its agrarian culture and natural surroundings. Deities were thought to be everywhere in nature, in the stars, mountains, rivers, animals, and even insects. Known as kami, they were believed to sustain all life. The kami were very accessible gods and were usually identified with a certain place where a shrine would be erected for worship.[91] Respect for parents has also been a strong component of Japanese culture, which further extends to a reverence for ancestors. The rituals and shrines that evolved to pay homage to the dead and kami eventually became known as Shinto, or the Way of the Gods. Shinto emphasized ritual and reverence rather than a complex moral code.

Buddhism came from China and spread rapidly. It seemed to satisfy certain religious needs of the people as well as political needs of the rulers. Early emperors decreed support for the Buddhist ethics of piety, peacefulness, and obedience, in effect embracing the support that Buddhism brought to the social order. Buddhist images and ceremonies were identified with the Shinto kami and were easily adopted. From China there also came an infusion of Confucianism with its rules of ethics and behavior. For centuries Buddhism and Confucianism have intertwined with native Japanese religious practices, evolving into uniquely Japanese sects.

An interesting episode relating to Japan's religious history occurred in 1281 when the Mongolian emperor Kublai Khan invaded the islands with an overwhelming force of over 150,000 men and an enormous armada. Although vastly outnumbered, the Japanese fought desperately against annihilation. They were saved by an unseasonable typhoon which scattered the invading fleet. This incident was considered an intervention by divine providence and became an important national religious heritage remembered as the Kamikaze—or Divine Wind.[92] It is interesting to recall two similar incidents in Chapter Two where the American army was saved from enemy fleets by unusual and fortuitous winds. The term *kamikaze* would later be applied to suicide pilots during World War II in the Pacific.

Christianity came to Japan in 1549 with the arrival of St. Francis Xavier, a Jesuit priest from Portugal. The Portuguese gained a foothold to trade in Japan due in large part to their introduction of firearms.[93] Growth in Christianity was dramatic with over 150,000 converts by 1580. Christians were concentrated in the Nagasaki area where the Portuguese were allowed to trade. During the 1580s other European traders began arriving and disputes began to break out between different groups. Accusations were made that much religious activity was being used for commercial advantage. There was also a certain amount of intolerance among the Christian community toward the Buddhist temples and priests. The Japanese rulers became increasingly unhappy with the discord. Christianity was banned in 1614, and, although the ban was not rigidly enforced, considerable persecution of Christians took place. Finally, in 1638, 37,000 Christians gathered on the peninsula of Shimabara behind fortifications in an effort to defend their freedom of worship. Armed forces were sent against them with a resulting massacre of all but a handful. In conjunction with this purging of Christianity practically all Europeans were expelled from the country, closing off contact with the Western world for over two centuries.

MODERNIZATION OF JAPAN

Japan couldn't avoid the attention of the outside world indefinitely. In 1848 the war between Mexico and the United States ended with American acquisition of western territories extending to California. Soon there was evidence of a new interest in the Pacific and Far East. For many years, shipwrecked fishermen and would-be traders had been handled rudely by the Japanese shoguns. Outsiders continued to be unwelcome. In 1853 Commodore Matthew Perry arrived in Tokyo Bay with a flotilla of four ships on an official U.S. government mission to gain an opening to Japan. By using a combination of military strength and diplomacy, Perry was successful in negotiating a treaty to open several ports and to establish an American consul. Within a few years other Western countries began to obtain similar concessions, signaling the start of a revolution in Japanese society.

By the 1870s a new political regime began to allow a pent-up interest in Western civilization to flourish, largely stimulated by the realization that modernization was essential to compete with the rest of the world. Over the next forty years one of the most dramatic changes to occur in any nation in history began to unfold. Japan began a process of reshaping itself using Western expertise in engineering, education, economics, law, and military organization. In 1889 a constitution was adopted using a European model with variations to suit the Japanese. Supreme authority was centered in the emperor. Considering the unique military influence within Japanese culture, and remembering American intimidation in 1853, the military was given special status in the government with direct responsibility to the emperor.

Rapid industrialization was accomplished through government investment and control of factories. The emphasis was on heavy industry and infrastructure to support an expanding military establishment. The latest concepts in Western military organization and weapons were assimilated. Universal conscription was initiated. During the late 1800s the Japanese were well aware of European colonialist expansion in Africa and Asia. The United States also established a presence in the Pacific, acquiring control of the Philippines and Guam after the Spanish-American War. The Japanese had logically concluded that military strength was the key to maintaining their independence from foreign domination and to expanding their own influence.

Japanese organizational skills were also focused on religion. In 1900 a Bureau of Shrine Affairs was created within the Japanese government to centralize control of priests and shrines.[94] An ideology was promoted at the national level emphasizing loyalty and worshipful devotion to the emperor as the direct descendant of the mythical sun goddess Amaterasu. This ideology was officially sponsored within the government, military, education system, and throughout society. The school curricula were shaped to promote an overt nationalism centered on the emperor. The aim of teaching history was to "foster a national spirit," and of geography to "instill love of country." Each of the boys were asked daily, "What is your dearest ambition?" The response was, "To die for the Emperor!"[95]

JAPANESE EXPANSION

As an island nation with limited natural resources and little arable land, Japan found England to be an ideal role model. England's great navy and historical trading expertise were supported by a colonial network circling the globe providing markets for manufactured goods and sources of raw materials. Japan looked initially to mainland Asia as the natural arena for such an empire of its own and fought wars against China and Russia to gain control of Korea and parts of Manchuria. When World War I began in Europe in 1914, Japan quickly declared war on Germany and seized German territory in mainland China and in the Pacific. Japan became an original member of the League of Nations in 1920 and was given a mandate over the Pacific islands taken from Germany.

By this time Japan had established herself as a world power and stood with the United States supreme in the Pacific. In America, Japan's expansion and methods were beginning to stir apprehensions. Within Japan a long-developing struggle between the civil and military authorities continued to simmer. The growing commercial classes were beginning to believe that Japan could compete in world markets for growth and power. The military continued in their long-held belief in Japan's right to acquire new territories by virtue of her strength and destiny. Unfortunately, at this critical juncture, the Great Depression descended on the Western nations, resulting in protectionist measures that severely impacted Japan's ability to trade in world markets.[96] Using its constitutionally established advantages within the government, the military high command began to assert increasing control over national policy.

In September 1931 Japanese army units occupied Manchuria. Although not sanctioned at the time by the Japanese government, neither was the move rescinded. In 1932 the new nation of Manchukuo was established under full Japanese control. As this major new source of raw materials was realized, the position of the military was further strengthened. The League of Nations denounced this action and refused to recognize the new state. Japan then withdrew from the League. In 1937 Japan initiated a war of conquest in China after a clash with Nationalist Chinese troops near Peking. The Japanese army rolled through China in a brutal campaign which included atrocities against hundreds of thousands of civilians.[97] The Japanese advance was slowed finally by the vastness of the territory conquered. By 1938 Japan was in control of most of eastern China, including Canton, Shanghai, and other coastal cities. The rest of China's coast was under blockade.

DIPLOMATIC RELATIONS BETWEEN JAPAN AND THE UNITED STATES

As Japan was conquering China, Germany and Italy were aggressively expanding their control of Europe. Isolationist sentiment continued strong in the United States, even though public opinion was against this aggression. While preoccupied with developments in Europe, President Roosevelt took the only actions available to him to deal with Japan. In July 1939 Secretary of State Cordell Hull gave the Japanese government required notice for abrogation of the Commercial Treaty of 1911, setting the stage for an embargo of strategic materials. This had major implications since the United States was Japan's major source of scrap steel and oil. There followed over a year of intense diplomatic activity as both countries sought a formula to head off the growing possibility of war.

As the diplomats talked, Japan, Germany, and Italy continued to act. Germany's invasion of Poland in September 1939 brought war in Europe with Britain and France. By June 1940 France had fallen. Within months Japan signed a formal alliance with Germany and Italy and moved troops into French Indochina. It appeared that Japan had the intent and capability of continuing conquests in Asia. In early 1941 a military conference was held in Washington between the United States and Britain, potential allies in an imminent worldwide war. Agreement was reached that Europe would receive top priority in such a war and that the United States would have secondary responsibility for the Pacific.[98]

Diplomatic negotiations between Japan and the United States continued to produce no results. Japan was committed to her plans for a "Greater East Asia Co-Prosperity Sphere," continuing to send forces to Indochina. Finally, in July 1941, the United States froze all Japanese assets and cut off the supply of oil. This precipitated the final crisis. Japan was faced with the choice of giving up all her gains, or of immediately undertaking the conquest of all Southeast Asia to ensure control of the resources needed for her economy and war machine.[99] In October the civilian government of Japan fell and the military under General Hideki Tojo took formal control. The Japanese diplomats were given a limited time for further negotiations. At that time Japan's oil reserves were being consumed at the rate of 12,000 tons a day. Also, the United States Congress had finally committed appropriations for building ships that would see Japan's naval superiority dwindle within several years.

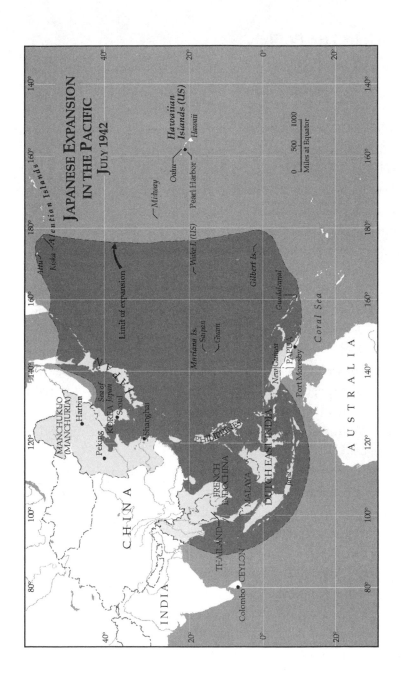

JAPANESE EXPANSION
IN THE PACIFIC
JULY 1942

Aleutian Islands

Attu

Kiska

Limit of expansion

Midway

Hawaiian
Islands (US)

Oahu

Pearl Harbor

Hawaii

0   500   1000
Miles at Equator

Wake I. (US)

Gilbert Is.

Mariana Is.

Saipan

Guam

Guadalcanal

Coral Sea

MANCHUKUO
(MANCHURIA)

Harbin

Peking

KOREA

Seoul

Sea of
Japan

JAPAN

Shanghai

CHINA

New Guinea

PAPUA

Port Moresby

AUSTRALIA

PHILIPPINES

FRENCH
INDOCHINA

THAILAND

MALAYA

DUTCH EAST INDIA

Java

CEYLON

Colombo

INDIA

WAR IN THE PACIFIC

On November 5, 1941, the Japanese high command decided to go to war within a month, barring an unexpected diplomatic breakthrough.[100] Ambitious plans had been finalized to seize all of Indochina, Burma, Malaya, the Philippines, Dutch East Indies, and Pacific Ocean islands covering a vast region. For years Japan had known that the United States would present the only obstacle to her plans. In war gaming, the Japanese Navy had generally concluded that the wisest course was to draw the American fleet into Japanese waters where a decisive naval engagement would be fought, reminiscent of their great victory at Tsushima in 1905. However, in 1941 Admiral Isoroku Yamamoto, commander in chief of the Japanese Combined Fleet, proposed a plan to strike the U.S. Pacific Fleet at Pearl Harbor in Hawaii before declaring war.[101] Japan had conducted a similar surprise attack at the outset of the war with Russia in 1905. Yamamoto believed that Japan could not wait for an American attack or for America to increase its naval strength. By destroying the U.S. Pacific Fleet initially Japan would achieve clear dominance in the Pacific for several years. With Axis success in Europe and Africa it was hoped that Japan could win the Pacific by default.

On December 7, 1941, six Japanese aircraft carriers launched a massive air strike against Pearl Harbor. All eight American battleships were moored in port and were caught totally unprepared. Four were sunk and four were severely damaged. Over three hundred aircraft were destroyed, mostly on the ground. There were 3,600 American casualties.[102] Of bitter disappointment to the Japanese, however, was the absence from port of all three U.S. aircraft carriers. The *Saratoga* was on the West Coast, the *Lexington* was delivering airplanes to Midway, and the *Enterprise* was returning from delivering planes to Wake Island. Also, overlooked in the strike were fuel farms near the harbor with over 4 million barrels of oil, the lifeblood of what remained of the U.S. Pacific Fleet.

On December 8th the United States declared war on Japan. Japan's allies, Germany and Italy, immediately declared war on the United States. America found herself facing adversaries victorious in all theaters of a war already well under way, with powerful and effective military forces. In the Pacific the Japanese fleet was superior in every category of shipping, especially with the U.S. battleship fleet rendered almost nonexistent. The three untouched American aircraft carriers still faced ten Japanese carriers with well-trained, veteran aircrews, and aircraft superior to any then available to the U.S. fleet. The United States Army, numbering only 190,000 in 1939, was frantically expanding for war.[103]

Almost simultaneously with the Pearl Harbor strike, Japanese attacks were launched against Wake Island, Guam, the Philippines, Thailand, Malaya, and the Gilbert Islands. All fell before the onslaught as the Japanese closed on the Dutch East Indies and the oil fields so vital to their war effort. British and American ships opposing the advance were sunk or driven off, buying only a little time. In the Philippines American bombers were destroyed on the ground, dooming any hope of defending those islands. In early March the conquest of Java and the Dutch East Indies was complete. Japan had accomplished all her immediate war aims in half the planned time and with virtually no naval losses.

THE UNITED STATES ON THE DEFENSIVE

After Pearl Harbor, Admiral Chester Nimitz was made commander in chief of the Pacific Fleet. His initial mission was to

USS Arizona Sinking at Pearl Harbor. (National Archives)

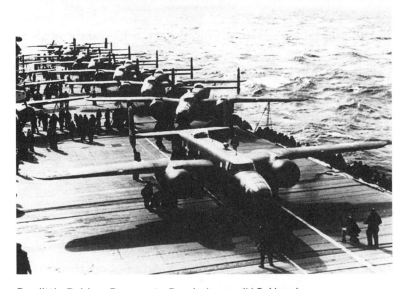

Doolittle Raiders Prepare to Bomb Japan. (U.S. Navy)

hold Hawaii and to maintain sea-lanes to the West Coast and between the West Coast and Australia. With three aircraft carriers and a limited number of supporting ships available, he could only hope to annoy the Japanese. In February and March single carrier task forces hit isolated Japanese-held islands in quick raids. On April 18 a more daring strike was undertaken against Tokyo by sixteen B-25 bombers taken into Japanese waters by the carrier *Hornet.* Although minimal damage was inflicted, a furor was caused within the Japanese high command that a strike had been allowed against the homeland.[104] Strategically, the Japanese had to face the need for defense of their own home waters for the first time.

In early May two U.S. carrier groups combined against a Japanese move threatening Australia. One of the carriers was the *Yorktown,* recently arrived from the Atlantic. In the ensuing Battle of the Coral Sea the Japanese lost one small carrier and sustained damage to the larger *Shokaku.* The Americans lost the *Lexington* and incurred one bomb hit on the *Yorktown.* Although the losses were more critical for the Americans, the Japanese invasion force bound for Port Moresby, New Guinea was turned back. With limited success so far in his holding mission and with few resources on hand or on the way, Nimitz had to await the next Japanese move.

One American resource that was to prove extremely important in coming months was the Combat Intelligence Unit of the 14th Naval District in Pearl Harbor code named "Hypo," and known within a very limited circle as the "Black Chamber." American intelligence had broken the Japanese naval code JN-25 in 1940, and Nimitz's Hypo unit was able to provide him with a wealth of information about Japanese fleet activity. Analysis of this information was not always easy or exact, and it would take some time to convince Nimitz of its reliability.

In April and May 1942 the Japanese high command went through a thorough analysis of strategic options.[105] Offensive operations could be continued southward toward Australia or westward toward Ceylon and India. Admiral Yamamoto argued for a turn to the east toward Midway Island and Hawaii. It had become clear to him that the remnants of the U.S. Pacific Fleet were still an effective fighting force, posing risks to his fleet and Japan. He knew that if the United States was allowed time to regroup and rearm, his country would be in trouble. He needed a decisive battle with the U.S. fleet. On May 5, 1942, the decision was made to attack Midway, with diversionary strikes in the Aleutian Islands. By striking to the east and thereby threatening Hawaii and even the U.S. West Coast, the Japanese hoped that Nimitz would be forced to react with all available forces. The job left undone at Pearl Harbor would be finished.

FLEETS CONVERGE ON MIDWAY

From May 26 to 28, 1942, the most powerful fleet seen so far in history sortied into the Pacific from anchorages in Japan and Saipan. The two hundred ships involved were organized into task forces: The Northern Force was assigned troops and ships to strike the Aleutian Islands. The Midway Force was to invade the island of Midway. The Carrier Striking Force, commanded by Vice Admiral Chuichi Nagumo, was to provide air support for the invasion of Midway and air power against enemy ships. This force included the aircraft carriers *Akagi*, *Kaga*, *Hiryu*, and *Soryu*. The Main Force consisted of seven battleships, including the flagship of Admiral Yamamoto, and carried the large-caliber naval guns to prevail in any surface engagement, then still considered to be the ultimate naval weapon. In all, Yamamoto was committing to the battle eleven battleships, eight carriers, twenty-two cruisers, sixty-five destroyers, twenty submarines, and additional troop and support ships. His main worry was that the U.S. fleet might not appear for the decisive battle that he hoped to bring about.

During May the tension began to build within the U.S. Pacific Fleet headquarters. The Hypo unit at Pearl Harbor was urgently trying to make sense out of increasing Japanese radio traffic. An objective area AF was frequently mentioned. There was a belief that this was a central Pacific location, although conclusive proof was lacking. Intelligence agencies in Washington were also busy trying to determine Japanese intentions. Some felt that Australia would be hit next; many thought Hawaii or California. Acting on their hunch, the Hypo unit had a plain text message sent out describing problems with Midway's water distillation equipment. Within a few days a Japanese message was intercepted that "AF has fresh water problems."[106] Apparently the riddle had been solved, if this was not an elaborate ploy on the part of the Japanese. As more detailed information on the timing and composition of the attack was deciphered, Admiral Nimitz decided to go with his Hypo unit.

Nimitz's first order of business was to assemble his available aircraft carriers at Pearl Harbor. The *Hornet* and *Enterprise* were recalled from the South Pacific, arriving on May 27 for two days rearming and refueling. The *Yorktown* limped into port a day later with extensive bomb damage sustained at Coral Sea. She had been at sea for one hundred two days, and her crew was nearly spent. It was estimated that necessary repairs would take ninety days. Three days were allotted. The attack was expected in the first few days of June. Any ship that would play a part had to be at sea. On May 29 Task Force 16 sailed from Pearl Harbor with Rear Admiral Raymond Spruance commanding the *Hornet*, *Enterprise*, six cruisers, and nine destroyers. A day later Task Force 17 put to sea commanded by Rear Admiral Jack Fletcher with the *Yorktown*, two cruisers, and six destroyers. All units were headed for a point

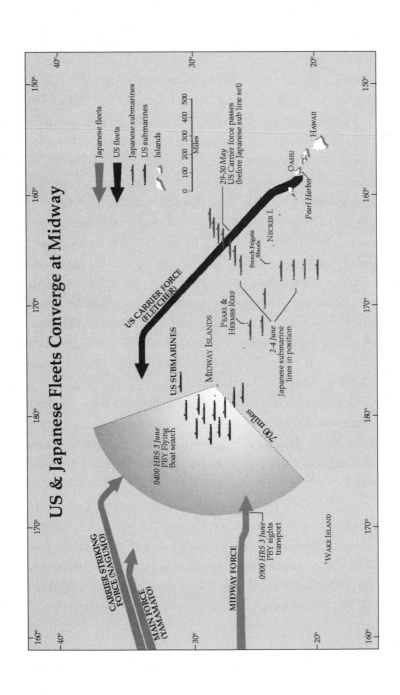

US & Japanese Fleets Converge at Midway

Japanese fleets
US fleets
Japanese submarines
US submarines
Islands

Miles
0 100 200 300 400 500

CARRIER STRIKING FORCE (NAGUMO)

MAIN FORCE (YAMAMOTO)

MIDWAY FORCE

0900 HRS 3 June PBY sights transport

"WAKE ISLAND"

0400 HRS 3 June PBY Flying Boat search

700 miles

US SUBMARINES

MIDWAY ISLANDS

US CARRIER FORCE (FLETCHER)

PEARL & HERMES REEF

2-4 June Japanese submarine lines in position

FRENCH FRIGATE SHOALS

NECKER I.

29-30 May US Carrier force passes (before Japanese sub line set)

OAHU

Pearl Harbor

HAWAII

northeast of Midway designated by Nimitz as Point Luck, where Fletcher would assume overall command.

MISSED OPPORTUNITIES

As the Japanese fleet advanced across the Pacific, the one thing that Yamamoto urgently needed was information. A long-distance aerial reconnaissance flight to Pearl Harbor by a four-engine seaplane was devised to fill some of this need. To cover the distance and reroute, refueling by submarine was required. The submarine *I-123* was dispatched ahead to an assigned location at a small island between Midway and Hawaii. On May 30 the *I-123* reported U.S. ships near the rendezvous point, necessitating a twenty-four-hour postponement.[107] The next day ships were still in the vicinity. Instead of attempting an alternate plan, the Japanese naval staff in Tokyo canceled the mission. There would be no overflight of Pearl Harbor.

It is possible that the Japanese did not persevere with the troubled aerial reconnaissance because of plans to deploy submarine lines between Hawaii and Midway to provide early warning of U.S. fleet movements. However, problems also plagued this operation. The submarines tasked to this mission had been on almost continuous patrol since the beginning of the war. Extensive overhaul was required which took two extra days. Also, some of the subs were involved in the aborted aerial reconnaissance refueling mission. One line of the submarine cordon took position on June 2, the other on June 4.[108] Both were late as Task Forces 16 and 17 by then had safely passed. As the climax neared, Admiral Yamamoto remained in the dark about U.S. fleet movements.[109] He continued to believe that he was unopposed for his initial operations against Midway.

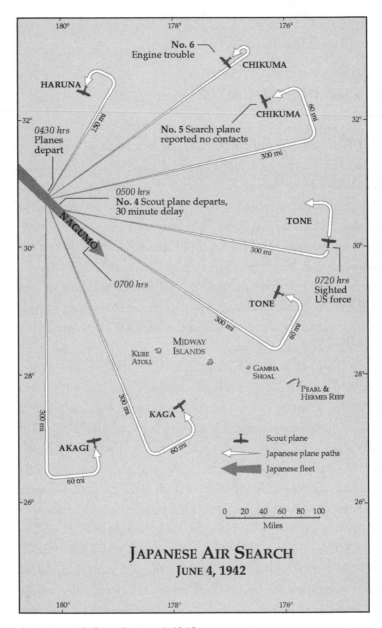

Japanese Air Search June 4, 1942

THE "FAILED AIR SEARCH"

All through the night of June 3-4, Admiral Nagumo's Carrier Striking Force steamed southeast toward Midway. As dawn approached he still had no information about the presence of enemy ships. Normal carrier tactics in this situation called for an aerial reconnaissance screen from the carrier force's own resources. Accordingly, at about 4:30 a.m. Nagumo put up his aerial search, fanning out in about a 180° arc from south to east to northeast. The southern portion of the arc was covered by two carrier planes, the eastern portion by two floatplanes from the cruiser *Tone*, and the northeastern area by two floatplanes from the cruiser *Chikuma* and one from the battleship *Haruna*. Six of these planes were to fly out three hundred miles, turn left for sixty miles, and then return. The *Haruna's* plane could only cover one hundred fifty miles. Amazingly, the Japanese air search was plagued by a series of mishaps in the sector where the U.S. fleet should have been discovered. One of the *Chikuma's* aircraft developed engine trouble and had to return to ship at 6:30. It was later determined that this aircraft would have flown directly over the American fleet.[110] Aboard the *Tone* mechanical problems were experienced with the ship's catapult. Her search planes were delayed a fateful thirty minutes in launching.[111] One of these would eventually spot the enemy just moments too late to save Nagumo from disaster.

OPENING MOVES—JUNE 4, 1942[112]

The first blow delivered against Midway was by Nagumo's Carrier Striking Force. Aircraft were launched at 4:30 a.m. for a 6:30 bombardment of the island. Half of the available aircraft were held back for defense of the carriers and to strike enemy ships in

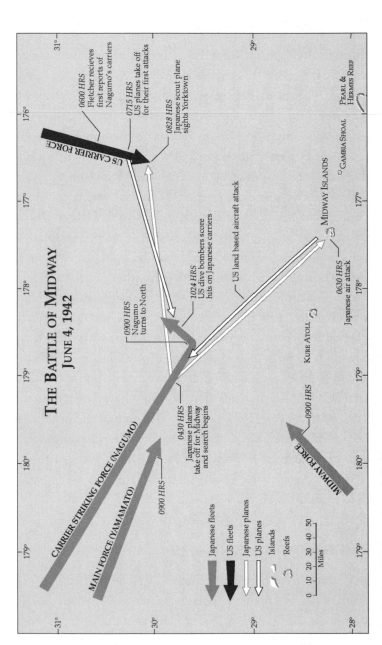

The Battle of Midway June 4, 1942

the unlikely event that any should be detected. PBY flying boats were already fanning out from Midway looking for the Japanese. At about 5:30 a PBY spotted the *Akagi* about one hundred fifty miles from Midway and reported enemy aircraft heading toward Midway. By 6:00 a.m. all land-based aircraft on Midway were airborne. The U.S. carriers immediately turned toward the reported Japanese position and prepared to launch aircraft at about 8:00.

The first wave of Japanese aircraft hit Midway at about 6:30 a.m., damaging buildings, fuel farms, and runways. All Midway aircraft, alerted earlier, were airborne and headed for the reported Japanese ships. Their attacks would achieve no hits but would keep Nagumo busy for over an hour. Since his scout planes had sighted no enemy ships, and all of the attacks against him were by land-based aircraft, Nagumo decided at 7:15 to rearm his remaining aircraft for a second strike against Midway. This rearming was about an hour-long process of switching torpedoes and armor-piercing bombs for contact-fused bombs suitable for land targets. As confusion reigned on the Japanese carrier flight decks and unsuccessful attacks continued by Midway aircraft, Nagumo received a startling message at 7:28 from the *Tone*'s scout plane #4: "Ten ships, apparently enemy, sighted."[113] Waiting anxiously for clarification of this report, Nagumo rescinded his order to rearm at 7:45. By this time the process was about half completed.

NAGUMO'S DECISION

At this point Admiral Nagumo was concerned about the presence of enemy ships, although there was still no sign of an enemy aircraft carrier or carrier airplanes. His force had been attacked by over sixty aircraft from Midway, including B-17 bombers, without a single hit on one of his ships. So far everything was going according to plan. At about 8:20 the first of his own aircraft from the dawn

TBD Devastator Launches Torpedo. (National Archives)

Dauntless Dive-Bombers at High Altitude. (U.S. Navy)

strike on Midway was overhead. All would soon arrive needing to land for fuel and ordnance. At this exact moment, another message arrived from the *Tone* scout plane: "The enemy is accompanied by what appears to be a carrier."[114] This report was a profound shock to Nagumo and every officer on the bridge of the *Akagi*.

Suddenly, Nagumo was faced with a momentous decision. Should he launch his available aircraft immediately to attack the reported carrier, or should he clear his flight decks and recover his returning aircraft? The bold move would have been to attack immediately. Several of his subordinates recommended this. However, an immediate launch would have sent an attack against the Americans without all aircraft armed properly and short of fighter cover. Also many of the returning aircraft were damaged and low on fuel. Delays in landing could have cost lives and aircraft. At 8:30 Nagumo decided to take the more cautious approach, ordering his flight decks cleared and all returning aircraft recovered. Aircraft were to be rearmed with torpedoes and armor-piercing bombs and preparations made for an all-out attack on enemy ships. The Japanese force turned to the north as crews worked feverishly to get ready.

SUCCESS OUT OF CONFUSION— THE "PERFECT ATTACK"

According to tactical principles of the time, a carrier air group was supposed to attack using a carefully coordinated procedure. Fighters would approach high overhead to deal with enemy fighters, opening the way for the torpedo planes at surface level and dive-bombers from high altitudes in steep bombing runs. As is often the case in combat, however, tactical principles were not applied on June 4, as the U.S. carrier attacks achieved virtually *no* coordination.

The thirty-five dive-bombers of the *Enterprise*, led by Lieutenant Commander Wade McClusky, flew their assigned heading searching in vain for their objective. They were not aware that the enemy ships had changed course. Nearing the limit of his fuel, McClusky knew that time was running out. At about 9:50 a.m. he spotted a lone white streak in the ocean. Using his binoculars, he saw what he thought to be a destroyer running at full speed. Guessing that the ship might be headed for the rest of the fleet, he turned that way. His guess would pay off within half an hour. The ship was indeed the Japanese destroyer *Arashi*, detached to pursue a submarine contact, and now on the way to rejoin the carrier force.

The first to find the Japanese carriers was *Hornet's* Torpedo Squadron 6. Unfortunately, their fighter cover was separated, and their dive-bombers never arrived. At 9:20 they gallantly commenced their long, painfully slow torpedo runs through curtains of antiaircraft fire and enemy fighter pursuit. All twelve aircraft were lost without damaging an enemy ship. From 9:35 to 10:20 the *Enterprise* and *Yorktown* torpedo squadrons also joined the attack without support and paid a similar price, with no results. In all, thirty-five to forty-five torpedo planes and crews were lost in this hour. Few times in war, however, has such apparently futile sacrifice achieved so much. As the Japanese carriers maneuvered to avoid these attacks, they could not launch their own aircraft. And, as the torpedo attacks kept coming despite their losses, all of the Japanese fighter cover over the fleet became engaged at low level. The attention of every shipboard gunner was focused on the spectacle of the attacking torpedo planes.

At 10:20 a.m., as the last torpedo plane staggered away, Admiral Nagumo ordered his ships to turn into the wind to launch aircraft. So far, his fleet had suffered no losses and had performed brilliantly. The moment had arrived for him to deliver the

decisive blow of the battle. At virtually that same moment, Lieutenant Commander McClusky looked down to see the Japanese
carrier fleet below him. As he watched the first Zero roll down
the flight deck and become airborne, he rolled his Wildcat over at
15,000 feet and led his dive-bombers down. Within minutes the
Yorktown dive-bombers also appeared. At this moment there was
no Japanese fighter opposition and for precious seconds no reaction by antiaircraft fire. Within two minutes the heart of Japan's
fleet was ripped out in one of the most decisive moments of this
or any war.

Akagi took two bomb hits, one in the middle of the flight
deck, and the other aft on the port side. Neither of these hits
would necessarily have been fatal. However, with a full flight deck
of armed and fueled aircraft, open gas lines, and ammunition
loose on deck, fires and secondary explosions spread unchecked.
Although the crew worked valiantly for hours to control the damage, *Akagi* was abandoned later that day and sank early the next
morning. The *Kaga* received four bomb hits with similar results
and sank by early evening. The *Soryu* was hit by three bombs
causing such destruction that she was abandoned within twenty
minutes. Only the *Hiryu* escaped this attack as she was separated
from the other carriers at the time. Later in the day the *Hiryu*'s
bombers would find and strike the *Yorktown*. Limping away, but
still under control, the *Yorktown* was further hit by submarine torpedoes and sunk. A short time later *Yorktown* and *Enterprise* dive-
bombers found the *Hiryu*, delivering four bomb hits which proved
fatal. With the loss of these four carriers and over three hundred
aircraft, the core of Yamamoto's Carrier Striking Force had ceased
to exist.[115]

Although in a state of shock, Yamamoto maneuvered his
fleet for two days trying to salvage something from the battle. He
was unsuccessful in getting his battleships or remaining aircraft

USS Hornet. (U.S. Navy)

Japanese Aircraft Carrier *Kaga.* (Govt. of Japan)

within striking distance of Nimitz's two remaining carriers. Even though he continued to possess numerical superiority in all classes of ships, mentally he was beaten. On the morning of June 7 the Japanese fleet set course for home.

AFTERMATH

The Battle of Midway was the clear turning point of the Second World War in the Pacific. With this defeat the Japanese lost their best and possibly only opportunity to win the war. The initiative was lost and never regained. A week after Midway the Imperial General Headquarters canceled plans to invade Fiji and Samoa, scheduled for July. Efforts went into strengthening the territories already gained, especially on the perimeter islands of New Guinea, the Bismarks, and Solomons. In August U.S. Marines landed on the little island of Guadalcanal in the Solomons, representing America's first offensive move in the Pacific. After a bitter six-month naval and ground campaign, Guadalcanal was finally taken in what proved to be the first step toward the Japanese homeland.

For years before the outbreak of World War II there had been a growing controversy within the U.S. Navy regarding the roles and importance of the traditional battleship fleet versus the new and untried naval aircraft carrier component.[116] This controversy was completely resolved for the U.S. Navy by the destruction of its battleships at Pearl Harbor on December 7, 1941. The decisive weapon of this war would be the aircraft carrier. This dispute was not resolved so cleanly by the Japanese as evidenced by Yamamoto's task organization at Midway. His battleships were designated the Main Force and were held to the rear in anticipation of the decisive engagement. Their awesome firepower never played a part in the battle.

By early 1943 the thing which Admiral Yamamoto had feared from the beginning began to happen: new *Essex* and *Independence* class aircraft carriers began arriving for duty with the U.S. Pacific Fleet. Before the end of 1943 the U.S. 5th Fleet was organized consisting of four fast carrier task forces with two heavy and two light carriers each, accompanied by escorting battleships, cruisers, and destroyers. These forces would achieve air and naval superiority across the Pacific as Marine amphibious units captured islands ever closer to Japan.

Before the end of World War II in the Pacific, many more bitter and bloody battles would be fought on islands and at sea. The Japanese war machine continued to be an awesome force even without the four carriers lost at Midway. They still had a superior navy and army, and a fighting spirit unequaled in most cultures. The losses at Midway were carefully concealed from the population that never wavered in its zeal to carry on the war. In many engagements the Japanese forces would prevail, and, up to the end, would fight to the last man rather than surrender any ground. After 1943, however, the Japanese were simply not able to keep pace with the United States in replacing ships, aircraft, troops, and, especially, trained naval pilots. Time and industrial capacity worked in favor of the United States, just as Yamamoto knew they eventually would. Instead of a victory at Midway and domination of the Pacific, the Japanese were faced with a long, defensive war that they were not destined to win.

GOD'S HAND IN WORLD WAR II

Of the wars discussed so far, the war against Japan gives me the most concern in speculating about God's purpose. As I have already confessed, I am no theologian and am very unqualified to present Christian theology, especially pertaining to other religions in the

Crash Landing on *USS Enterprise*. (National Archives)

world and to people throughout the world who have not been exposed to the Christian gospel. I am also not an expert on the Shinto and Buddhist religions, and the multitude of sects that have blended to form Japan's rich and complex religious heritage. It is my own belief that God, in his compassion, provides for every human being who seeks a relationship with him, no matter the form of worship. I do not believe that this was in any way a religious war, or that God's purpose was for Christianity to prevail because of any precedence over Shinto or Buddhist religious culture.

I do believe that Japanese aggression can be cited as the proximate cause of World War II in the Pacific. I have tried to present enough information about historical events leading up to the war to show that Japan certainly had many perceived justifications for its actions. The European powers pursued their own interests in Asia during the nineteenth century, as did the United States. Japan felt it had to compete, and that military strength was necessary to be competitive and to defend itself. Its geography and cultural evolution gave Japan an unusual history of isolation and a unique nationalism. Never has history seen an entire nation transform itself so quickly and effectively as did Japan during its period of modernization. Unfortunately, there was a dark side to this process. As the military establishment became the dominant force in Japan's government during the early 1900s, Buddhism was separated from Shintoism by government edict, in effect creating a national religion based on devotion to the emperor.[117] I don't believe that the required worship of a human emperor as a civic duty was pleasing to God. Nor do I believe that God looked favorably on the channeling of this religious "faith" toward the attainment of a social order and national goals of expansion as devised by Japan's military leaders.

In considering European colonialism and American acquisition of new territories, Japan cannot be entirely faulted for her own visions of empire. For decades, Japan had asserted her national interests in Manchuria, Korea, and other mainland Asian areas close to her shores. It may not be possible now to speculate on how much expansion was too much. However, I believe that at some point in the 1930s Japan did cross a line. Her concept of areas of vital interest expanded to the point of including all East Asia.[118] Military conquest was her method of expansion, often with unnecessary ruthlessness. Within Japan personal and religious freedoms were constrained. In her conquered territories freedom was snuffed out. I believe that this aggression and oppression were not in keeping with God's will and that God's hand moved to bring it to an end.

On the surface, America's victory in the Pacific during World War II might seem to have been inevitable in light of the disparity of resources. The story presented so far should dispel this illusion. In 1942, Japan's military forces were superior in the Pacific and close to total domination. If what was inevitable had then occurred, the Japanese Combined Fleet would have swept away the remnants of the U.S. Pacific Fleet on June 4, 1942, and Japan would have continued its imperialistic expansion that had gone on uninterrupted for over forty years. With no effective U.S. naval presence in the Pacific, Yamamoto's battleships and aircraft carriers would have had free reign to strike anywhere, including Australia, Hawaii, and even California.

Japan apparently had no specific plan to invade the United States. The goal of the war was to gain American acceptance of Japanese hegemony in Asia with a cessation of American interference. They came very close to achieving this goal. Who can guess what the position of the United States would have been if San Francisco and Los Angeles had come under the 16-inch naval guns of Yamamoto's battleships? Perhaps some diplomatic solution might have finally been found allowing Japan a freer hand. If nothing else, the "Europe first" strategy would have been out the window. United States attention would have been immediately focused on its own West Coast and the Pacific. If the Axis powers had then been defeated in Europe, Russia would have had a larger role and would undoubtedly have controlled more of Europe after the war. A democratic West Germany and France would have been in doubt. It is difficult to speculate on all the scenarios that might have flowed from a Japanese victory at Midway. However, even though such a victory was as close to a sure thing as any student of military history can imagine, it was apparently not in God's plan that it should happen.

It is hard to believe that America was ever in danger of conquest during World War II, although this conclusion comes mainly in looking back from our present perspective. At the time, most

Americans were fearful of what would happen throughout the world, including America, if Germany, Italy, and Japan continued triumphant on all fronts, as was the case up until mid-1942. There were indeed some very dark days for America during these early war years. My own mother was a coast watcher during World War II and helped staff a lookout tower in Myrtle Beach, S.C. She was trained in German and Japanese aircraft and ship recognition. There was widespread apprehension over the possibility of invasion. Who knows what direction Axis war planners would have taken if America had become truly isolated, without allies in Europe and naval strength in the Pacific. I believe that God was clearly working to protect America and her allies during this war from the aggression that was moving unchecked against them.

When I started to research church history prior to and during World War II, I expected to find that Christianity in America would have been especially dynamic during this period. My own experience growing up in a small Southern town in the 1940s formed this expectation. Practically every person that I knew was a member of a Protestant church and generally serious about participating in church affairs. This seemed true of every small town within my limited sphere. It was surprising to learn that this was not the pattern everywhere else in the nation. Although religious belief continued strong in middle America during the 1930s and '40s, there were growing currents running in a different direction. New advances in science since the early 1900s increasingly brought many religious beliefs into question, especially within the scientific and academic communities. Communism and Socialism began to take root during this era as many intellectuals sought more effective solutions to society's problems than those offered by existing political and religious institutions. Many abandoned the churches altogether believing that science held the key to all-important questions of life. Rifts began to appear within many churches between fundamentalists, clinging to the traditional word, and liberals, intent on modernizing the church to make it more compatible with new ideas. Many of these divisions continue today. In spite of these developments, however, I believe that America continued basically to function in accordance with God's plan. America continued to be the one place on earth where individuals were free to pursue their own understanding and worship of God without coercion or interference. I know that during World War II millions still turned to God with faith in his protection. I believe that God heard these pleas and continued to bless America.

GOD'S HAND AT MIDWAY

As we consider the events leading up to the Battle of Midway and the battle itself, we see another critical moment in American history when the fate of this nation and others turned on what has been considered by many to be completely random luck.

The book titled *Midway, The Battle That Doomed Japan* has been cited frequently as a source throughout this chapter. Written by two Japanese naval officers, it has a Foreword written by Admiral Raymond Spruance, in which he makes this comment:

> In reading the account of what happened on 4 June, I am more than ever impressed with the part that good or bad fortune sometimes plays in tactical engagements. The authors give us credit, where no credit is due, for being able to choose the exact time for our attack on the Japanese carriers when they were at their greatest disadvantage—flight decks full of aircraft fueled, armed and ready to go.[119]

Admiral Spruance displays a sense of humility unique to a military hero. Without any reference to a higher power he at least concedes the point that the actions of the leaders involved did not govern the outcome of events on that day. There are times, often crucial times, when commanders do not have control of battles and when men don't even have control of their lives. This should be a humbling realization in itself. To me, this realization leads further to the belief that in many situations it is actually God's hand that is in control.

Many books have been written about the Battle of Midway and many analyses done of the reasons for the outcome. Much credit is properly given to the intelligence victory achieved by the Hypo unit at Pearl Harbor, giving Admiral Nimitz valuable insights into Japanese intentions and dispositions. Much blame is given to Admiral Yamamoto for the dispersion of his ships and failure to concentrate his forces at the crucial point. He is also criticized for failing to regroup after his initial setback and for not aggressively resuming the battle. There are many other specific factors contributing to the outcome of this battle. The American commanders seemed to combine prudence and boldness exceptionally well. The American airmen performed magnificently with inferior aircraft and weapons. Although God's hand might not be so clearly evident in all of these human actions, there would be no reason to rule it out.

In one sense the U.S. intelligence advantage at Midway was irrelevant. The Japanese were attacking Midway for the specific purpose of decisively engaging what was left of the U.S. Pacific Fleet. An overabundance of naval power was deployed to ensure that whatever the Americans sent to defend Midway would be overwhelmed. Yamamoto's main concern was truly that the American carriers would not show up at all. As the operation unfolded, Yamamoto and his commanders knew that up-to-date information on enemy ship movements was vital, and plans were laid to provide this information. At every stage this effort was plagued by remarkable bad luck. The flying boat reconnaissance of Pearl Harbor had to be canceled due to problems at the refueling site. Both submarine patrol lines were late arriving due to the flying boat refueling problem and to maintenance delays in Japan. Nimitz pushed his carriers out to sea in a hurry because he didn't know when the Japanese were going to strike, not to foil Yamamoto's submarine screen.

As dawn approached on June 4, the Japanese were still unaware of the American carriers. This deficiency should have been remedied by the normal air search screen put out by Admiral Nagumo at 4:30 a.m. The procedure for such a screen was well perfected by this point in the war, and no naval commander would have operated in enemy waters without such early warning protection. Nagumo's screen did find the American ships, although moments too late to avoid disaster. In considering the problems encountered by the Japanese with the failed air search, we begin to strain the concept of bad luck. Mechanical problems with the *Tone*'s catapult cost a fateful thirty-minute delay. What would have been the effect of a report to Nagumo at 7:00 a.m. of the presence of enemy carriers? Similarly, the *Chikuma*'s scout plane, which would have passed over the U.S. fleet, was forced back with engine problems. To me this incredible sequence of Japanese failures to discover the presence of the American carriers has to be more than bad luck. Any sighting of an American carrier by any Japanese ship, submarine, aircraft, or spy in Hawaii, on any day before June 4 or before 7:00 a.m. on June 4, would have produced a totally different outcome to this battle. I have to believe that God's hand was at work to prevent this happening.

God's most decisive influence on events can be seen later in the morning of June 4. Combat is always confused and confusing, and very little ever goes according to plan. Such was the case on this day. At 10:20 a.m., out of the total chaos raging in the skies and seas around Midway, came the two-minute "Perfect Attack." The Japanese carriers' decks were full of fueled and armed aircraft. In spite of the confusion and delays, every available aircraft was ready for the decisive strike against the American fleet. Practically every U.S. torpedo bomber had been shot down. Most of the U.S. carrier planes were lost. After trailing a lone destroyer wake for half an hour, the dive-bombing squadron from the *Enterprise* finally arrived, unopposed at high altitude by Japanese air cover. Destruction of the Japanese Carrier Striking Force was sudden and complete. It would be practically impossible to devise a logical scenario where destruction of three aircraft carriers would be possible within so few minutes. It would have to strain anyone's imagination to believe that so much "luck" was possible in connection with one event. At the time, Nimitz and Spruance undoubtedly did feel that fortune was on their side. In retrospect I believe that we can clearly see God's hand at work in the Battle of Midway.

In a speech given a few months after the battle, Chester Nimitz said, " . . . I am convinced that there comes a time when every leader entrusted with the safety of his country finds faith in God the ultimate inspiration for victory."[120] He went on to say years later that, "The security of this country is not a material thing but rather rests in the spirit of the people. . . . We are a people with faith in reason and God."[121] These statements were made by a man not known for regular church attendance.[122] I believe that during his time of trial by fire and ultimate triumph Nimitz saw much more than his own skill or luck at work, and that his faith was strengthened by his experience. I think that in looking back on these events, with all of the data at hand as to what actually happened, we must be in even greater awe of what God accomplished.

They go out to the kings of the whole world, to gather
them for the battle on the great day of God Almighty.
They gathered the kings together to the place
that in Hebrew is called Armageddon.

—REVELATIONS 16:14, 16

CHAPTER FIVE

THE COLD WAR– BRINK OF ARMAGEDDON

O N OCTOBER 16, 1962, *President John F. Kennedy
was given conclusive proof that Soviet nuclear missiles
had been placed in Cuba, threatening American cities
throughout the eastern United States. After a series of secret meetings
with his advisors, Kennedy made an address on national television
publicly demanding removal of the missiles and proclaiming a naval
blockade of Cuba. As the tension built each day, the fact became obvious that any aggressive act could easily lead to escalating reactions on
both sides. Each side had nuclear weapons and had threatened to use
them. If the United States and the Soviet Union were to go to war over
Cuba, could either side afford to lose such a war without using every
weapon available? The world suddenly faced the single most dangerous
moment in its history. Many wondered if God's hand was moving the
world toward the prophesied day of Armageddon.*

WORLD WAR II ENDS—
THE COLD WAR BEGINS

On April 25, 1945, American and Russian forces came together at Torgau, Germany, virtually completing the conquest of Nazi Germany. Unconditional surrender followed within days, as separate occupation zones were established in Germany by the victorious Allied powers. By July, Franklin Roosevelt was dead and Winston Churchill voted out of office, leaving Joseph Stalin of the Soviet Union as the last great wartime leader in power. Stalin had wielded absolute authority in the Soviet Union since 1929. His nation had endured invasions and devastation before, and it was his aim to come out of this war with expanded frontiers and buffer zones to ensure the security of the Soviet Union in the future. The Soviet Union had suffered the greatest losses of the war, and at war's end also had the largest army in the world, hardened by years of heavy fighting. As the other victorious nations sought to end the war and return to normalcy, the Soviets looked to their own interests and pursued their own aims.

During the closing months of the war, Soviet forces "liberated" the Eastern European countries of Hungary, Poland, Bulgaria, and Rumania from Nazi occupation. It had been agreed among the Allied powers at the Yalta conference in January 1945 that the Soviet Union had a rightful sphere of influence in Eastern Europe. It was further agreed that free elections would soon be held in these countries. This of course did not happen as Communist parties, with Soviet military backing, took over political control. To the dismay of the United States and Western Europe, severe restrictions on travel and trade with the West were imposed as Eastern Europe came under complete and seemingly permanent domination by the Soviet Union. By 1946 Winston Churchill would lament the growing situation with the famous words:

From Stetten in the Baltic to Trieste in the Adriatic, an iron cur-
tain has descended across the continent. Behind that line lie all
the capitals of the ancient states of Central and Eastern Europe.
Warsaw, Berlin, Prague, Vienna, Budapest, Belgrade, Bucharest,
and Sofia—all these famous cities and populations around them
lie in what I must call the Soviet sphere . . . this is certainly not the
liberated Europe we fought to build up.[123]

As the Soviets consolidated their hold over Eastern Europe,
confrontations with the West began to occur in other areas. Ter-
ritorial disputes broke out with Norway and Turkey. Violating an
agreement with Britain, Soviet forces remained in Iran after the
departure of British troops. Communist insurrection threatened
Greece. It became more and more apparent that Soviet expansion-
ism was not completely defensive in nature.

As the strongest world power emerging from World War II, it
fell to the United States to counter these Soviet moves. Harry Truman assumed the presidency of the United States after Roosevelt's
death. Reflecting a war-weary nation, he used diplomatic pressure
as much as possible to resolve these disputes. However, he began
to find that diplomatic effort needed the backing of a U.S. military
presence in many areas of the world. In 1947 Truman announced
to Congress a new foreign policy committing the United States
to assisting any nation economically and militarily that requested
aid in resisting Communism. This policy of containment became
known as the Truman Doctrine.

The newly emerged superpowers were entering into a decades'
long struggle which would become known, often inappropriately, as
the Cold War. Berlin, China, Korea, Hungary, Indochina, and other
critical areas would become the focal points of conflict, each in their
own turn. By the early '60s center stage would shift to the United
States' own backyard as Communism gained a foothold in Cuba.

CHRISTIANITY IN THE UNITED STATES

The end of World War II seemed to usher in a new era of religious consciousness in the United States. The uncertainties and perils of four long war years had profound effects. There were countless family separations, anxieties, and losses. Families at home were often without husbands, fathers, and other loved ones as they worked and sacrificed in support of the war effort. Millions of servicemen faced separation and loneliness, and a large proportion serving in combat areas faced physical hardship and danger. It has been said that there are "no atheists in a foxhole." I believe that this was often true during World War II where many served aboard ship or in combat units for as long as the war lasted, unless they were sooner wounded or killed. During the war six hundred chapels were constructed on military bases, and over 8,000 chaplains were on duty ministering to the needs of the troops.[124] Most servicemen and civilians were conscious of the fact that they were fighting for America's freedoms and that important among these was the freedom of worship. For every family with loved ones surviving and returning home there was much to be thankful for.

After the war, families were reunited, postponed marriages consummated, and the baby boom created. Prosperity flourished for many as the industrial capacity of the United States was reoriented from war production to the satisfaction of pent-up consumer needs for housing, cars, and everything else imaginable. As the only industrialized nation in the world untouched by the physical devastation of war, America was blessed with vast economic potential and optimism about the future. It would take years for the reality and danger of the Cold War to sink in and only as its monopoly on atomic weapons disappeared and the Korean War started, would new anxieties appear in America's consciousness.

A religious revival flourished during the late 1940s and 1950s as church membership grew twice as fast as the population.[125] Church attendance soared, contributions mounted, and new churches were built in record numbers. Religious books became popular. The *Revised Standard Version* of the *Bible* broke all records for book sales in 1950. Norman Vincent Peale became a popular success. His book, *The Power of Positive Thinking*, attracted a large following with its mixture of religion and psychological self-help. In 1954 Congress added the words "Under God" to the Pledge of Allegiance and in 1955 adopted "In God We Trust" (on coins since 1864) as the official motto of the United States. A young evangelist named Billy Graham came to the attention of the public after a series of successful tent meetings in Los Angeles where several prominent personalities were publicly converted to Christianity. Graham became the most widely heard Christian evangelist of all time, eventually reaching every continent with a global ministry.[126] The scope of his success was due in part to the growing mass media of radio and television, which seemed to be supportive of religion during this period.

There are reasons to suspect a certain superficiality in America's religious fervor of this period, in light of the trends undercutting religion during the prewar years already mentioned in Chapter Four. There was certainly a concurrent mushrooming of materialism as the consumer society moved into high gear after the war. Developments in science and technology continued to lead many away from organized religion, and the apparent success of Communism seemed to offer a system that promised material gain for the masses of humanity living in economic misery. Not only was God not needed in this system, he was seen as a negative force draining support away from the dedication required by the system itself.

CHRISTIANITY IN THE U.S.S.R.

The Russian Orthodox Church has been the predominant religious institution of Russia for over a thousand years. Its influence within the Soviet Union has been centered in the Russian, Byelorussian, and Ukrainian Republics. From the beginning the church was allied with the secular power of the tsars and supported the doctrine of royal divine right and ordination. The church cooperated fully with the state in a system of total autocratic rule and grew in power over the centuries with the throne.[127] From the beginning of the Soviet state in 1917, the church came under attack as the communists consolidated all power within the government. Vast holdings of church property were confiscated, and clergy were placed at the lowest order of society. Religious publications, religious education outside the home, and, especially, evangelism were made impossible through regulations. Religious institutions were considered rivals for the absolute loyalty of the citizenry and were allowed to exist in an uneasy state of subjugation to the state. During Stalin's purges of 1936–39, 95 percent of the 100,000 existing places of worship were forcibly closed, and the ranks of the clergy were decimated by murder, exile, and prison.[128] The evangelical churches, the largest being the Baptist, fared better under Communism due to the fact that they had always been outside the religious establishment, and already had to cope with discrimination and even persecution from the tsars and Orthodox Church itself. They were adept at organizing small groups for Bible study and prayer meetings, and the clergy had been forced to blend in with their followers, holding regular jobs and living among their followers.

The churches enjoyed a respite during World War II as Stalin and many church leaders found that religion could play an important role in building support for patriotism and the war effort. It is estimated that 20,000 churches were allowed to reopen, and clergy control of church property was restored.[130] This respite continued until Stalin died in 1953 and was a unique hiatus in the otherwise unbroken history of Communist-church antagonism.

Under Nikita Khrushchev's regime, organized religion was brought back forcefully under party control and active persecution. In 1960 regulations were published confining the clergy to strictly spiritual matters with church governance assigned to parish councils, usually controlled by local party officials. Over the next three to four years over half the established parishes were disbanded and 10,000 churches closed.[131] According to one historian:

> Clergy were classified according to the degree to which they were "loyal to socialist society" . . . What (was) valued in priests and bishops was inactivity, a purely formal attitude to divine services, readiness to preach Soviet patriotism, the party's social policy and participation in the international peace movement. The Soviet state, in other words, was no longer trying to destroy the church, but to use it as a pliant instrument.[132]

It is difficult to assess the effect of this continuing state of religious persecution on believers in the Soviet Union. An untold number abandoned their religious practices and even their spiritual beliefs in the face of this well-organized and in many cases violent repression. However, it is also known that a significant number responded in a different way altogether. They went underground to continue worshipping and to pursue their faith at an even deeper level. More clergy abandoned their official status in the church and took up secular pursuits, sharing life more closely with their congregations. These gatherings in many respects took on the form of the early Christian church, where small groups came together under dangerous circumstances. As Christ taught his followers, "Blessed are those who are persecuted because of righteousness . . ."[133] There have been millions of Soviet citizens who have suffered for their beliefs and have undoubtedly been blessed by a deeper relationship with God.

THE ARMS RACE

Underlying the postwar conflicts between the Western democracies and Communism were new and ominous weapons. On August 6, 1945, the United States had dropped an atomic bomb on the Japanese city of Hiroshima with the blast equivalent of 12,000 tons of TNT, instantly demolishing everything within a half-mile radius of ground zero and causing severe damage beyond. Such destructive power delivered by one bomber on one mission brought a radically new dimension to warfare. At this time the United States was the only country in possession of such a weapon. With this monopoly, the United States proceeded with an almost total demobilization of its conventional forces after World War II. By 1947 American armed forces were down to 1.5 million from wartime levels of 12 million. In 1949 however, the Soviet Union tested its first atomic bomb, completely changing the strategic balance of power, and starting an arms race that would continue to escalate.

As the atomic bomb was being developed in the early '40s there had been speculation among the physicists involved that a more powerful weapon was possible. It was theorized that the energy of an atomic detonation could be used to set off a reaction in heavy hydrogen, resulting in an explosion of far greater magnitude. At the end of World War II, development of this weapon was set aside. The Soviet atomic test brought this issue back to life. A heated and divisive debate ensued within the scientific community. Many wanted no part in developing such a weapon. In the blast of the

atomic bomb one scientist perceived a glimpse of the apocalypse—
"in the last milli-second of the earth's existence, the last man will
see what we saw."[134] The position of the military and many others
in government was that the United States could not afford to let
the Soviets gain any advantage in development of this technology.
The issue came to the desk of the president, who, in January 1950,
finally ordered initiation of a project to develop a "Super" bomb.

In 1952 the United States detonated the first hydrogen
fusion weapon of 10.4 megatons, equivalent to 10.4 million tons
of TNT.[135] This weapon could totally destroy an area within 4
miles of ground zero and cause severe damage out to ten miles.
Radioactive debris and fallout could blanket vast areas depend-
ing on atmospheric conditions. The Soviets followed a year later
with a test detonation of their own hydrogen bomb. In succeeding
years both countries began stockpiling nuclear weapons seeking to
gain an advantage over the other. In 1957 the Soviets successfully
tested a long range ballistic missile and then launched Sputnik,
the first space satellite, seemingly gaining an advantage in the ability to deliver nuclear weapons at great range. The United States
immediately accelerated its Minuteman solid fuel intercontinental
ballistic missile (ICBM) and Polaris submarine missile programs.

The existence of these weapons systems had a profound
effect on relations between the United States and the Soviet
Union, now referred to collectively as the superpowers. From
the period of the Korean War onward, during every Cold War
confrontation, each side had to calculate the possibility of escalation that could lead to the employment of these weapons.
Winston Churchill wrote in 1955 that there was "an immense
gulf between the atomic and hydrogen bomb. The atomic bomb,
with all its terrors, did not carry us beyond the scope of human
control or manageable events . . ."[136] The hydrogen bomb did go
beyond human control and even threatened the existence of

humanity itself. A Third World War was almost unimaginable. Albert Einstein was asked how such a war would be fought. He answered that he had no idea how a nuclear war would be fought, but that the war after that would be fought with stones.

CASTRO

In 1959 events in Cuba began to unfold that would bring the superpowers to their most dangerous confrontation and the world to its most dangerous moment. Since 1953 a group of revolutionaries led by Fidel Castro had fought against the dictatorial government of Fulgencio Batista. Over time the rebels gained in popular support and extended their control over ever-larger areas of the country. The situation came to its climax at midnight on January 1st as Batista fled Havana and the way was opened for Castro and his forces.

Although Castro himself was not then a Communist, his brother Raul was a secret member of the Cuban Communist party, the Partido Socialista Popular (PSP). Control of the Cuban military forces fell to Raul, who secretly sought Soviet bloc advisors and military aid to consolidate the position of the new government. These requests found their way to Khrushchev and the Politburo, who agreed to limited, secret support. The PSP had been underground in Cuba since 1952 and had little support among the Cuban people.[137] With Raul in power there was hope for Communist inroads into the new government, although any move had to be very carefully planned.

Castro was suspicious of the United States, which had always had vast economic interests in Cuba and extensive influence over the Cuban economy. Also, the American government had generally backed Batista during the years of Castro's struggle. Castro's early political moves were to institute agrarian reform under the direction of PSP members and to nationalize U.S. owned sugar properties.[138] Alarm bells began going off in Washington. In early 1960 President Eisenhower authorized CIA planning for covert operations against Cuba. As tensions grew, Castro began to fear a U.S. invasion, leading him to seek more military support and closer relations with the Soviets. This process reached an ominous milestone on July 9, 1960, when Khrushchev announced Soviet nuclear retaliation if Cuba were subjected to armed intervention.[139] Castro was delighted with this overt display of support. In October he moved to nationalize other sectors of the Cuban economy and continued eliminating private property rights. On November 8, 1960, two days after the election of John F. Kennedy to the U.S. presidency, Castro declared to his inner circle that he was a Communist.[140]

KENNEDY

During the 1960 presidential campaign, John Kennedy had brought Cuba to the forefront as a political issue. Seeking to offset Richard Nixon's reputation in foreign affairs, Kennedy attacked Republican foreign policy in general and claimed that Cuba was the most glaring failure of all. He advocated the ouster of "Castro and his gang." As he took office after a very close election, he had to ensure that Cuba was high on his agenda.[141] Unfortunately, by then, the U.S. had no diplomatic relations, very little trade, and practically no leverage over Cuba. An outright invasion was considered unacceptable due to unfavorable world opinion and to other efforts in progress to arrange an early summit meeting with the Soviets to address larger issues such as arms control and Berlin. Khrushchev's nuclear umbrella over Cuba also could not be ignored.

On March 16, 1960, Kennedy approved more or less by default a covert CIA plan aimed at Castro's overthrow. A brigade of Cuban exiles would be landed in Cuba at the remote Playa Giron (Bay of Pigs) to seize territory for the establishment of a new government and coordination of an anticipated uprising against Castro. The president insisted that there be no overt U.S. military involvement. This stipulation necessitated cancellation of U.S. air support over the invasion beaches, allowing the small Cuban air force to disrupt the landings and to destroy supplies and ammunition before reaching shore.[142] By April 19 Cuban military forces had defeated the invaders and had captured practically the entire force. Kennedy was forced to accept responsibility for a humiliating setback. Cuba had become a political thorn in his side that his Republican opposition was not going to let him forget.

Other developments compounded Kennedy's political problems. On April 12 the Soviet cosmonaut Yuri Gagarin completed the first manned space flight, another Soviet technological breakthrough following their earlier Sputnik success. In Southeast Asia the communist Pathet Lao were making gains in their effort to take the Laotian capital of Vientiane. Desperate for some foreign policy success Kennedy and his advisors focused on a summit conference scheduled for Vienna in June 1961. Kennedy and his brother, Robert, worked diligently through formal and informal channels to ensure that some agreement on arms control could be reached. Aware of Kennedy's vulnerability, Khrushchev decided to be tough, avoiding arms control and demanding his own way on Berlin. Kennedy was frustrated in his efforts and to a degree even humiliated at Vienna, where nothing of substance was achieved.[143]

KHRUSHCHEV

Nikita Khrushchev appreciated Kennedy's problems as welcome relief from his own. Under his regime, Soviet economic development, especially agriculture, continued to lag chronically. Rather than addressing underlying economic factors, his typically Communistic approach was to work on the administrative structure, striving for ever greater discipline and efficiency.[144] More bureaucracy and big military budgets served to undermine economic progress. On the international scene Berlin continued to be a sore point as a free world enclave in the middle of Soviet occupied eastern Germany. Getting nowhere in negotiations, he built the Berlin Wall in August 1961 to stem the flow of East Germans into free Berlin. This solved one set of problems but was a propaganda disaster with the rest of the world. China was causing friction within the Communist bloc by its criticism of Soviet leadership in the Third World. The Chinese favored a more confrontational approach and more support for revolutionary movements everywhere. Khrushchev had to worry about the Soviet position in Cuba since Castro could turn to the Chinese for support at any time.

Especially critical to Khrushchev was the world's perception of Soviet military strength. During the presidential campaign of 1960, Kennedy had seized on the apparent Soviet superiority in space and long-range rocket technology, criticizing the Eisenhower administration for allowing the United States to be on the short end of a "missile gap." Nixon did not respond to this charge, fearing that disclosure of the true picture would spur greater Soviet efforts. Khrushchev was delighted with this situation. As long as the perception of Soviet superiority was there, he could continue diverting scarce resources toward solving economic rather than military problems. In fact, however, Soviet strategic forces were lagging badly behind the United States.[145]

The Soviets had been forced to cancel production of their highly publicized first-generation ICBM due to design flaws. By 1961 a better system was being built although only sixty-four were deployed compared to two hundred American ICBM's.

Compounding this disparity were another two hundred U.S. intermediate-range ballistic missiles (IRBM's) stationed in Europe, and superior U.S. long-range bomber and nuclear submarine assets.[146] Khrushchev knew that it would take ten years of big military budgets to redress an over four to one imbalance in nuclear weapons.[147] So, he continued to rely on bluff and misperceptions. Even though he desperately wanted progress in arms control talks, he could not concede an inch on the constant U.S. demand for inspections, which he knew would reveal the true situation. A speech by an assistant secretary of defense rebutting the existence of the so-called missile gap stirred Khrushchev to a drastic response. He ordered an atmospheric test of the largest hydrogen weapon ever built.[148] On October 30, 1961, a 50-megaton device was detonated over the Soviet Arctic.

THE MISSILE DECISION

At some point in early 1962 Khrushchev began to see a convergence of several of his problems and possible solutions in Cuba. If he were to send Soviet nuclear weapons and missiles to Cuba, this one bold move could reassert his own leadership at home, establish Soviet leadership vis-à-vis China, defend Cuba against U.S. intervention, and redress the imbalance in strategic nuclear forces. Although the Soviet Union had never stationed ballistic missiles outside its own borders before, the United States obviously had no problem with this concept as it had already taken steps to defend its allies in Europe with nuclear capable missiles. In 1961 Jupiter missiles had been placed in Turkey, across the Black Sea from Russia, aimed, according to Khrushchev, at his own dacha.[149]

Since mid-1960 the Soviets had already supplied over $250 million in military supplies to Cuba, including tanks, artillery, aircraft, and ships. Training was being provided in Eastern Europe and in Cuba by three hundred Soviet advisors. This increased Soviet presence in Cuba was of course a concern to Washington. Establishment of a Soviet armed base was considered unacceptable; although no one could articulate the point at which growing Cuban defensive measures should precipitate a response, or what the response should be. Kennedy asked his military advisors to develop contingency plans.

On April 9, 1962, it was announced that President Kennedy would personally attend Lantphibex-62, the largest Atlantic-Caribbean military exercise ever held. Forty thousand troops and eighty-four ships were involved in amphibious landings at beaches in North Carolina and Vieques Island, less than fifty miles from Cuba. The Cubans and Soviets took this as a clear warning. On April 12, 1962, Khrushchev and the Presidium decided to up the ante even more. The scheduled delivery of four divisions of SA-2 antiaircraft missile launchers was advanced. It was also decided to supply four cruise missile launchers, ten Il-28 medium bombers, and a 650-man contingent of Soviet soldiers with a Soviet general officer in charge. Concerned with the defense of at least three possible invasion areas, Castro asked for even more of everything.

As Khrushchev weighed the problem of defending Cuba and the cost and time to reestablish some semblance of strategic balance in ICBM production, the idea of sending nuclear capable missiles to Cuba gained momentum. By May 20 Khrushchev had made the decision. He proceeded to forcefully present his idea to the defense council and to the full presidium. He stressed that he did not expect these weapons to be used, but that he intended to scare the United States, "giving them a little of their own medicine."[150] He wanted absolute secrecy until November 6, after the U.S. elections. By then he believed that Kennedy would be faced with a fait accompli and be forced to accept the situation.

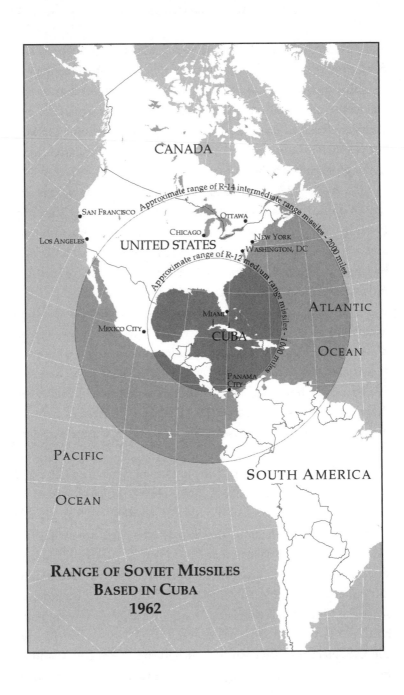

RANGE OF SOVIET MISSILES
BASED IN CUBA
1962

Although some would later denounce his "adventurism," Khrushchev was given the presidium's unanimous approval on May 24. Negotiations followed within days to gain Castro's approval. Reluctant at first, Castro quickly warmed to the idea. He soon objected only to the secrecy, feeling that the world should know how Cuba would be defended.

OPERATION ANADYR

Measures went ahead to ensure total secrecy of the movement of military equipment to Cuba. The operation itself was code named Anadyr for a Siberian air base, giving the impression that this was the destination of the military equipment being assembled in Soviet ports and the eighty-five ships involved in the movement. The nuclear assets were impressive:

+ Three missile regiments armed with twelve R-12 medium-range ballistic missiles (MRBMs), each capable of delivering a total of thirty-six 1-megaton warheads to a distance of 1,000 miles.
+ Two missile regiments armed with twelve R-14 intermediate-range ballistic missiles (IRBMs), each capable of delivering a total of twenty-four 1-megaton warheads 2,000 miles.
+ Two cruise missile regiments with a total of eighty FKR cruise missiles with 5.6- and 12-kiloton warheads and a range of one hundred miles.

Other forces included twenty-nine Il-28 light bombers, a MIG 21 fighter wing, four motorized infantry regiments, and twenty-four SA-2 surface-to-air missile units with 144 launchers. In all, over 50,000 Soviet military personnel were to be sent to Cuba. The Soviet navy also started planning for a submarine base to accommodate at least seven vessels each equipped with three R-13 missiles with 1-megaton warheads.[151]

Operation Anadyr commenced in mid-July 1962, as ships began departing eight different Soviet ports.[152] The Soviets knew that they were entering a vulnerable phase due to American surveillance of their shipping and the likelihood that such an increase in activity would be noticed. Khrushchev's military advisors anticipated that U-2 aerial reconnaissance aircraft would definitely detect the missile sites in Cuba in spite of all their efforts at secrecy. Khrushchev chose to downplay this problem assuming that it would come too late to matter and that Kennedy would not have the backbone to take decisive action. Here Khrushchev was misled by his own lack of understanding of the American political system and the pressures that could be brought to bear on a president by his opposition.

Deception efforts were also initiated through diplomatic channels. Under the assumption that the Americans would know in general that a military buildup in Cuba was in progress, Anatoly Dobrynin, the Soviet ambassador, was instructed to tell the White House that the Soviets would do nothing before the upcoming congressional elections to "aggravate the tension in the relations between our two countries."[153] Georgi Bolshakov, a Soviet intelligence officer on the Soviet embassy staff, had become a favorite means of back-channel communications between Robert Kennedy, his brother, and the Soviet leadership.[154] Bolshakov was instructed to assure Robert Kennedy that any buildup in Soviet arms in Cuba was purely "defensive" in nature.[155]

U.S. REACTION

As Operation Anadyr moved ahead, the increased Soviet activity was soon apparent. U.S. naval forces tracked Soviet shipping

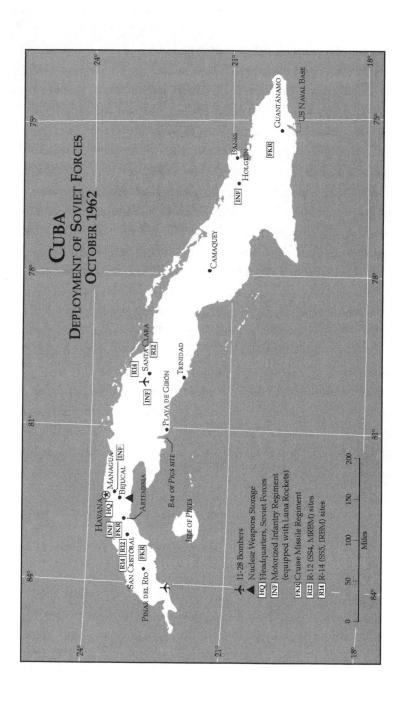

Cuba

Deployment of Soviet Forces
October 1962

24° 75° 78° 81° 84° 18°

San Cristóbal
Pinar del Río
San Cristóbal

Havana
Managua
Bejucal
Artemisia

INF HQ FKR INF R14 R12 FKR

Bay of Pigs site
Playa de Girón
Isle of Pines

R14 INF Santa Clara
R12 Trinidad

Camaquey

INF Holguín
Banes
FKR

Guantánamo
US Naval Base

✈ Il-28 Bombers
▲ Nuclear Weapons Storage
HQ Headquarters, Soviet Forces
INF Motorized Infantry Regiment
   (equipped with Luna Rockets)
FKR Cruise Missile Regiment
R12 R-12 (SS4, MRBM) sites
R14 R-14 (SS5, IRBM) sites

Miles
0   50   100   150   200

to Cuba, detecting a 50 percent increase in July over June.[156]
In August fifty-five ships arrived in Cuban ports, a fourfold
increase over the same month in 1961. CIA sources were providing reports of increased Soviet military personnel and cargo being
unloaded under conditions of maximum security. On August 29
a U-2 flight found eight SA-2 (antiair) missile sites in western
Cuba, the first evidence of any Soviet missiles on the island. These
weapons were a threat to all aircraft, including the U-2. Hoping to
avoid a political crisis, President Kennedy ordered an immediate
clampdown on this information, even within the CIA itself. U-2
flights were ordered cut back to prevent any public "incident."[157]
Kennedy was later criticized for being preoccupied with the coming elections and not wanting to give the Republicans a political
issue. His defenders argue that he justifiably tried to prevent a
political storm foreclosing his options.

Kennedy got a political storm anyway. Congressional Republicans were getting enough information on the Soviet buildup to question the president's actions. On August 31 Senator Kenneth Keating
accused the administration of willfully neglecting events in Cuba,
citing "reliable" reports of missile bases under construction. Public
anxiety over this possibility was now inevitable. On September 4,
Kennedy issued a statement through his press secretary attempting
to clarify conditions in Cuba that his administration would view as
grave threats. Specifically mentioned were Soviet military bases and
offensive ground-to-ground missiles. A few days later 150,000 men
in the U.S. Ready Reserves were called to active duty.

This response from Washington caught Khrushchev off
guard.[158] The Soviet buildup and Cuba itself were as vulnerable as
ever to any U.S. offensive action. Soviet strategic nuclear weapons
would not be operational until mid-October. He had invested far
too much of his own and Soviet prestige to abort the operation.
Khrushchev found himself in a position where acceleration of the

buildup seemed to be the only viable option. To counter the possibility of a U.S. invasion he focused on the one means that could be
put into place quickly: tactical nuclear weapons. On September 7 he
made the decision to speed delivery of eighteen tactical warheads in
the 8–12 kiloton range.[159] These weapons could be employed immediately by light bomber or short-range rocket and were intended to
destroy ship and troop concentrations. Khruschev pesonally gave
the Soviet commander in Cuba authority to use these weapons if
hostilities were started and communications with Moscow were
severed. Written orders to this effect were drafted, but were held in
Moscow.[160] There is no evidence of Khrushchev considering at this
point the consequences of being the first to use a nuclear weapon
against an opponent with nuclear weapons of his own.

During September the Kennedy administration considered
its options as the Soviet buildup continued. Covert operations to
weaken Castro had proven ineffective. As apprehension grew within
the CIA and Defense Department, military preparations intensified. Pressure mounted on the president from many sides. In early
October Cuba's president, Osvaldo Dorticos, asserted before the
United Nations that "We are well equipped to defend ourselves,"
and that Cuba could "become the starting point of a new World
War."[161] On October 10 Senator Keating made allegations on the
Senate floor that he had evidence of six ballistic missile launch sites
under construction in Cuba. Kennedy didn't know where this information came from, or even whether or not it was true. The time was
past for a cautious approach to U-2 overflights.

THE MISSILES ARE DISCOVERED

At 11:30 p.m. on October 13, Major Richard Heyser took off
from Edwards Air Force Base, California, for the first direct overhead reconnaissance flight of Cuba in six weeks. On the morning

Soviet Missile Site in Cuba. (National Archives)

Soviet Ship *Kasimov* with Missiles. (National Archives)

of October 16, photographs were waiting for the president showing medium-range ballistic missile sites under construction in
the San Cristobal area of west central Cuba.[162] Without inter-
rupting his schedule during the day, Kennedy began informing
the Executive Committee of the National Security Council, soon
to be referred to as ExComm. This group consisted of representatives from the Defense Department, State Department, CIA,
other cabinet members, and, of course, Bobby Kennedy. In strict
secrecy, ExComm was charged with the task of figuring out what
the president should do in response to this crisis. Air, ground, and
naval forces began moving in accordance with contingency plans
to do whatever the president might decide.[163]

Over the next five days Kennedy and ExComm confronted
this problem under pressure-cooker conditions in constant fear of
a premature public disclosure and political firestorm. On October
18 Kennedy met with the Soviet foreign minister, whose silence
on the missiles seemed to confirm the Soviet deception. Not
knowing his own plan of action, Kennedy did not raise the issue
himself.[164] He passed up the last opportunity to quietly disclose
what he knew and at least give Khrushchev an opportunity to
back down without a public loss of face. Some form of showdown
was the only course left open.

ExComm focused on four options, any one of which could
involve killing Soviet troops, and any one of which could prove to
be the opening stage of World War III:

1. Limited air strikes against missile sites.
2. General air strikes against the missiles and other military
   targets.
3. Invasion.
4. Naval blockade.

At first, Kennedy was committed to air strikes and plans proceeded in that direction.[165] However, on October 19 he was briefed by the Joint Chiefs of Staff (JCS), who had to point out that air strikes could not guarantee destruction of all the missiles.[166] Although there was no unanimous recommendation, several strongly advocated an immediate invasion. There was a general consensus that the Soviets would not start a nuclear war over Cuba. The president was not convinced. At no point did there seem to be any consideration of the possibility of tactical nuclear weapons in Cuba or the effect of their employment against invasion forces.

THE PUBLIC CRISIS

Consensus was finally reached to implement the blockade option. Some felt that this accomplished little with risks equally as great

John F. Kennedy and Nikita Khrushchev. (National Archives)

as the other options. Most, however, felt that a naval blockade would confront the Soviets, but still leave room for a de-escalation of tension. Of course it could also easily lead to further escalation. It would be up to Khrushchev. He would at least have the opportunity to respond constructively.

At 7:00 p.m. on October 22, 1962, President Kennedy went on national television to explain the crisis and to announce a naval blockade or quarantine of Cuba. He informed the nation and Moscow that the United States "would regard any nuclear missile launched from Cuba . . . as requiring a full retaliatory response upon the Soviet Union." He also said, "We will not prematurely or unnecessarily risk the costs of worldwide nuclear war . . . but neither will we shrink from that risk at any time it must be faced."[167] Both superpower leaders were now on record threatening to use nuclear arms over Cuba. The American public was suddenly jolted out of a vague anxiety about the Cold War and brought face-to-face with the acute threat of World War III.

As the President was speaking, all U.S. military commands worldwide were alerted and placed in Defense Condition Three (DefCon 1 being a state of actual war). Preparations were undertaken to implement the blockade, to invade Cuba if so ordered, and to fight a worldwide nuclear war if necessary. The Strategic Air Command went to airborne alert placing sisty-six nuclear loaded B-52 bombers constantly in the air. Army and Marine Corps units began moving to east coast ports to await embarkation. Blockade force ships not already at sea began moving out of Norfolk.[168] Khrushchev and the presidium moved immediately to increase the alert level of Soviet and Warsaw Pact forces. The Soviet embassy in Washington cabled Moscow that secret documents were being destroyed. Within the next few days newspaper articles would appear addressing civil defense procedures, bomb shelters, and food supplies.[169] A terrified world waited and prayed.

On October 24 the blockade went into effect as Americans were glued to their television sets. The quarantine zone was set along an arc drawn five hundred miles from the easternmost tip of Cuba, the range of Cuban combat aircraft.[170] One hundred eighty-three ships of the U.S. Atlantic Fleet were on station and ready. According to navy intelligence there were twenty-two Soviet surface ships and three known submarines en route to Cuba.[171] The *Aleksandrovsk* beat the blockade by hours with her cargo of nuclear weapons. It was anticipated that the Soviet freighters *Kimovsk* and *Poltava* would be the first ships to encounter the blockade, and intelligence indicated that both carried ballistic missiles. The freighters were expected to reach the quarantine line by the evening of the 24th, where the destroyer *Lawrence* and carrier *Essex* had been tasked to intercept and to board if necessary. It did not become necessary. A wave of relief flooded over the world

President Kennedy Meets with Members of ExComm. (National Archives)

as the Soviet ships gradually slowed and then reversed course. Unfortunately, the euphoria was short lived as the White House soon learned that only fourteen of the twenty-two Soviet ships had turned back.[172] The crisis was not over.

THE SECRET CRISIS

As the blockade went into effect, Khrushchev, with the approval of the full presidium, drafted a scathing letter to Kennedy rejecting "the arbitrary demands of the USA," and calling the quarantine "an act of aggression . . . pushing mankind toward the abyss of a world missile-nuclear war."[173] He vowed to take whatever measures might be necessary to protect the rights of the Soviet Union. He was aware at that time that all of his R-14 missiles and warheads were safely in Cuba. His order to turn the other ships away was less a peace gesture than an effort to safeguard precious nuclear assets from the U.S. Navy.

Over the next three days tensions mounted dramatically. At sea a deadly game of cat and mouse was being played out between five Soviet submarines armed with nuclear torpedoes and an array of U.S. Navy antisubmarine ships and aircraft. My own ship, the aircraft carrier *Randolph*, patrolled with her destroyer screen and embarked aviation units, including helicopter and fixed wing submarine trackers. The Soviet submarines were located and followed relentlessly. After days of dogged pursuit, several were forced to the surface, in effect losing the deadly game. Cargo ships began to approach the quarantine line. The tanker *Bucharest* was intercepted, hailed, and eventually allowed to pass as the White House debated what to do.[174] The captain of the Soviet-chartered *Collangatta* responded to a challenge with "Go to Hell" and steamed through the line.

One Soviet-flagged surface vessel, the *Marcula,* was stopped and searched in mid-ocean by a boarding party from the USS *Pierce.*[175] Every encounter at sea had the potential of triggering the escalation that all feared could not be stopped.

In Washington and Moscow, Kennedy and Khrushchev seemed to be carried forward by events that they couldn't control. Each leader was receiving conflicting advice and confusing information from distant and often-questionable intelligence sources. They were separated by seven time zones and long delays in the limited communications that were taking place. As time went by pressure increased on Kennedy to do something. The blockade had achieved a small success, but the missiles were still in Cuba. On October 26 he was briefed by the CIA that construction of missile sites was moving ahead rapidly.[176] With each hour the Soviet position was getting stronger, and the pressure for military action was getting more insistent. It has to be remembered that Kennedy had pledged to do something about Castro and had been totally frustrated in his efforts. Many of his advisors had hoped for some clear provocation to justify U.S. military intervention. For them the time for that intervention had arrived.

In Moscow, Khrushchev continued to receive information on American war measures. He was briefed when SAC went to Defense Condition Two, the highest state of alert for U.S. strategic forces short of war. A report was received that U.S. hospitals were preparing for mass casualties. Cables were coming from Cuba warning of an imminent invasion. General Issa Pliyev, the Soviet commander in Cuba, had already been given the authority to arm his nuclear missiles.[177] Khrushchev suddenly found himself dealing with the question of whether or not to release authority to use these weapons. He was becoming convinced that the U.S. was really going to war.

A STEP BACK

Over these few days the Cold War conflicts that had gone on for fifteen years seemed to be snowballing toward a climax. Kennedy and Khrushchev had both come to a point where no one had been before, with the continued existence of their countries and possibly the world subject to the decisions they were about to make. Each knew the effect of a 1-megaton nuclear detonation. But who could really imagine this destruction multiplied several hundred times? Each had overseen the buildup of these so-called strategic forces and had publicly threatened the other with their use. The advisors of each seemed able to deal with the risk of taking actions that might lead to the use of these weapons. However, when the burden of decision finally reached the two men who were solely responsible for the consequences, there was a pause—and evidence of a deep urge to avoid the final step. Finding a way out became more urgent than "winning." Difficulties in communication and the momentum of events would make this an extremely fragile process.

Khrushchev took the first step. At some point between October 24 and 26 he apparently decided in his own mind that he would have to sacrifice his own scheme to project Soviet strategic power to the Western Hemisphere. On October 26 he wrote Kennedy a letter offering to remove the missiles in exchange for a guarantee not to invade Cuba. This was followed by a further stipulation that U.S. missiles in Turkey be removed. Although this proposal offered the first ray of hope to the White House, there was no agreement within ExComm over what to do about it. Most felt that any agreement to trade missiles in Turkey would be a political disaster for Kennedy, afraid of any charge that he might have "backed down" in the confrontation. Also, at the time the proposal was received,

USS Randolph at Sea. (U.S. Navy)

U-2 Spyplane in Flight. (U.S. Air Force)

construction work on the missile sites was still ongoing. An alarming report had also been received from the FBI that Soviet diplomats in the United States were burning their files.

BLACK SATURDAY

Deliberations over Khrushchev's proposal were proceeding cautiously and slowly by various diplomatic and back-channel means, when the crisis was forced to a new peak on Saturday, October 27. In Cuba, Castro was convinced that the expected invasion was imminent and gave the order to fire on any U.S. aircraft penetrating Cuban airspace.[178] In the early morning hours Castro visited General Pliyev in an agitated state. Pliyev understood Castro to call for a first nuclear strike to preempt the invasion.[179] This was immediately cabled to Moscow. Pliyev also cabled that "In the event of U.S. air attack . . . we will employ all available means of air defense."[180]

During the morning of October 27 wartime conditions seemed to erupt in Cuba, as Cuban anti-aircraft batteries began shooting at low-flying U.S. reconnaissance aircraft. Even though the Cubans didn't hit anything, the Soviets thought hostilities had started. At about 10 a.m. Soviet radar detected an American U-2 high-altitude reconnaissance plane entering Cuban airspace at 70,000 feet. A request to engage the target quickly went up the chain of command. The Soviet air commander, Lt. Gen. Stepan Grechko, was the man on the spot. Unable to reach Gen. Pliyev, but aware of his cable to Moscow, he gave the order to fire. At 10:22 three SA-2 missiles were launched, destroying the aircraft and killing the pilot, Maj. Rudolph Anderson.[181]

When this news reached the White House and ExComm, it seemed that the final crisis had arrived. Established U.S. policy required retaliation if a U-2 was fired upon by a Soviet missile. For this mission, sixteen U.S. aircraft had been on thirty-minute

alert for days. Unless the SA-2s were destroyed, allowing continued U-2 surveillance, the United States would be blind as the crisis continued.

A few hours later I stood on the bridge of the USS *Randolph*
watching aircraft flares going off in the night sky. The Soviet Foxtrot class submarine that we had tracked for days finally broke
the surface. Our ships and aircraft were on station with weapons
ready, just as we knew the Soviets were armed and ready. I wondered at that moment if this was how World War III was going
to start. Many in the White House had the same thoughts, won-
dering if they would see the dawn of a new day. Families of some
insiders actually began evacuating Washington.[182]

I never knew how dangerous this moment was until years
later it was revealed that the Soviet Foxtrot class submarine that
we faced down had carried a nuclear torpedo. Under the stress
of low oxygen levels, high temperatures, and lack of communication with the outside world, the Soviet commander had actually
ordered the nuclear device armed. The *Randolph* was the target.
Somehow, the other officers on board the submarine persuaded
the captain to surface first, a fatal move if we had then been at war.

At this point in the crisis Bobby Kennedy was tasked by
the president with an urgent mission. That evening the president's brother met privately with Anatoly Dobrynin, the Soviet
ambassador.[183] He was visibly agitated, alluding to the fact that
the United States and U.S.S.R. were at a point that could lead
to an escalation that might be impossible to control. He put forward terms for a settlement, guaranteeing no invasion of Cuba for
removal of the Soviet missiles. He offered a deal to remove U.S.
Jupiter missiles in Turkey within four months. However, this had to
be a secret understanding and not part of any written, official agreement.[184] He ended with a request for a fast and clear response from
Khrushchev, through Dobrynin, before events pushed the crisis

beyond anyone's power to control it. President Kennedy somehow continued to withstand the urgent pressure to authorize air strikes against Cuba. He decided that he could at least wait until Sunday.

On Sunday morning, October 28, Khrushchev grimly acknowledged news of the U-2 incident. From his perspective, this was an event that could well give the military powers in the Pentagon the upper hand over Kennedy. For that reason he had warned Castro not to use his anti-aircraft guns, and now one of his own commanders had initiated a missile attack. The situation in Cuba had taken a very dangerous turn. Castro himself seemed to be losing control, apparently recommending a nuclear strike against the Americans. At noon Khrushchev began a meeting with the presidium, followed shortly by the arrival of Dobrynin's report. Dobrynin conveyed his impression that the American president was under severe pressure from the Pentagon to act and that there was little time left to resolve the crisis. Khrushchev called for a stenographer and dictated a response agreeing to "dismantle the arms which you described as offensive." He also drafted a secret message confirming the deal to remove the missiles in Turkey. At 5 p.m. (9 a.m. eastern standard time) Radio Moscow publicly announced Khrushchev's acceptance of Kennedy's proposal to end the crisis. In Cuba, Castro was enraged as General Pliyev was ordered to begin dismantling the missile sites. The crisis was over.

AFTERMATH

Nikita Khrushchev was considered the "loser" in this confrontation, as it was perceived that he had folded under the pressure. Making the first move cost him dearly. The general in charge of Operation Anadyr was dismissed, and an investigation was launched into the failures of Soviet intelligence during the crisis. Khrushchev maintained that he had actually achieved a victory with Kennedy's agreement not to invade Cuba. He had, however, given up a very costly bid to achieve strategic parity with the United States and would pay the price in increased defense budgets and poor economic performance over the next two years.[185] In 1964 he was ousted from power in a bloodless coup by his subordinates who brought charges against him, including his failure in Cuba.[186]

John Kennedy's approval ratings soared above 70 percent as the public reacted favorably to his apparently cool determination in facing down the Soviets. Most of the media went to great lengths to confirm this image, generally avoiding the fact that Cuba had been abandoned to the Communists. Kennedy had pledged to do something about Castro, and, in the end, had completely given up this effort. Of course neither the media nor Kennedy's critics knew about the deal to remove U.S. missiles in Turkey, which Khrushchev amazingly cooperated in keeping secret. Both Kennedy brothers had placed the secret deal and their political futures in the hands of the Soviet leadership to get out of the crisis and to achieve their "victory." This never became an issue as their careers were, unfortunately, short lived. Ironically, Castro would survive both superpower leaders in office, and Cuba itself would outlast the Soviet Union as a Socialist state.

The Cuban Missile Crisis did not bring an end to the Cold War. Conflict would continue for three decades at varying levels of intensity. The United States would endure its longest and most frustrating war in Vietnam and continue to fight insurgencies elsewhere attempting to contain Communism. Although the Cold War did not end, the Missile Crisis did represent its climax in regard to direct superpower confrontations. There would never be another showdown with the threatened use of nuclear weapons. In 1963 an atmospheric test ban agreement was signed and the famous hotline installed between the White House and the Kremlin.

In fact the Cold War would never be won at all, as the Soviet Union would go through a long process of self-destruction due mainly to philosophical contradictions in its own Communist ideology. The economic disparity between the Soviet Union and the West became more acute as the Communists continued trying to fine-tune their central controls, seeking more efficiency and discipline. In 1985 the relatively young Mikhail Gorbachev came to power and tried for the first time to address the underlying issues holding his country in poverty by allowing more freedom and economic incentive. He was eventually unable to control the forces that he let loose. Communist governments were swept out of power in Eastern Europe, including East Germany, where the Berlin Wall came down in 1989—a momentous milestone in the rebirth of freedom. The end of the Soviet Union itself came on December 8, 1991, as Boris Yeltsin and other leaders issued a statement: "We, the Republic of Belarus, the Russian Federation, and Ukraine, being members of the USSR and signatories of the Treaty of Union of 1922 . . . state that the USSR, as a subject of international law and a geopolitical reality, ceases to exist." In its place a Commonwealth of Independent States was formed. The Cold War, as the world had come to know it, was finally over. America stood alone as the world's only superpower.

GOD'S HAND IN THE CUBAN MISSILE CRISIS

Finding evidence of God's hand in the Cuban Missile Crisis has been a long process of study and prayer. I was involved in this event myself and have naturally had an interest in it ever since. I have always known that the world came close to disaster during those days in 1962. However, at the time that I started to seriously research this event, I did not know of any incident comparable to those presented in previous chapters, such as the 'Unopened

Note' or the 'Lost Order,' and had no idea what I would find. I have gradually reached the conclusion that this crisis played out largely in the minds of two men, as confusing events swirled around them. The U-2 crisis and the USS Randolph/Soviet submarine incident brought the crisis to a climax that finally enabled a resolution.

I have generally avoided discussing the thoughts and decisions of leaders themselves, since, even though I might see God's hand at work, the skeptic could point to other natural influences. I know that I haven't conclusively proven anything in this book, but I think that it would be most difficult of all to prove that God caused a particular decision. In Chapter Two I presented the Battle of the Virginia Capes as an example of a battle with such a miraculous outcome as to demonstrate God's hand in the various decisions and events that produced it. I believe that the Cuban Missile Crisis presents an even more dramatic example of God working in this way, in what was probably the most pivotal event in human history. It took a miracle to break the momentum of events that were leading toward a world-ending catastrophe. In this miracle we see the evidence of God's hand in the decisions of the two men and in the events that affected them.

No one will ever understand the mind of Nikita Khrushchev. The reasons for his decision to place nuclear weapons in Cuba have been explained and are clear. He clearly underestimated the young U.S. president whom he considered too weak to stand up to him. However, in the darkest hour of the crisis, when he decided to give up an important strategic undertaking in which he and his country had invested so much, what went on in his mind is still a mystery. He was probably surprised at Kennedy's tough stand, and he always had to consider the general inferiority of his own strategic forces. Even so, he was a proud and determined man who prided himself on his own toughness. In contrast to Kennedy, who he described as "the son of a millionaire," he was a miner and a metal fitter, and a self-made man. He had committed his nation to a course of action that he had laid out himself, for which he had unanimous support, and about which he had weighed the risks for months. His determination is evident in his own words, emphasizing his understanding of the possibility of a nuclear war:

> Great casualties would be inflicted on the United States. America would bring down fire upon itself. The missiles that had already been installed would strike New York, Washington, D.C., and other . . . centers. If there was war, casualties would be inflicted on the Soviet Union as well. But my point is, for the United States it would be a different war—different from World War I and World War II, when the Americans didn't even hear a rifle fired in anger. Americans don't know what an exploding bomb or artillery shell really means. They have fought in foreign lands, but here they were asking for fire on their own heads, and what a fire—from thermonuclear bombs![187]

At one point Khrushchev knew the risks and was ready to take them. He knew that weakness was the cardinal sin of a Soviet leader, and that bargaining away his missiles and undercutting an ally would be perceived as weak. I don't believe that this was a weak leader, and it seems improbable that he suddenly woke up to some new risk that he hadn't thought of before. So what could have led to a turnaround of this magnitude? Many things happened in Khrushchev's mind to lead him to this turning point. I believe that we have to consider the possibility of something beyond logic and purely rational decision making.

As John Kennedy began his presidency, he had great plans for his administration. At the top of his foreign policy agenda were U.S./Soviet relations and, especially, arms control. However,

Cuba continued to divert him from his larger agenda by taking center stage, usually at very inopportune times. He had of course made a campaign issue of Cuba himself and was compelled to do something about it.

"Something" turned out to be a series of covert activities under the general supervision of the CIA, including the Bay of Pigs fiasco. These covert operations made no progress in weakening Castro. As frustrations over Cuba mounted and Soviet support increased, it became apparent to many that an invasion was the only answer. Pressure on the president began to build.

The discovery of Soviet missiles in Cuba seemed to be the final straw and ultimate opportunity to "solve" the problem. All preparations were made during the largest mobilization of U.S. forces since World War II. Kennedy knew that his own strategic forces were superior to the Soviets, and that his invasion forces were ready in overwhelming strength. He had the stronger hand in this confrontation, and Cuba was in his own backyard. Politically, he could not afford to appear weak on Cuba or the Soviets, with elections only weeks away and his Republican opposition hounding him at every turn.

Kennedy knew that making an agreement to give up the option of invading Cuba would be viewed as a weak response. If information were to leak about the deal to remove Turkey's missiles and, in effect undercutting NATO, the reaction would be even worse. How could Kennedy expect this part of the deal to remain secret?

The strategic and political calculations that went through his mind at the critical moment are as unfathomable as those of Khrushchev. He did what most would now agree was the right thing. However, his decisions then to take no military action during the crisis and to give up his chance to resolve his own stalemate in Cuba were even more amazing than the change of direction taken by Khrushchev. Here again, I believe that the improbable actions of one of the two principles involved in this crisis shows the likelihood that something was playing a role in this situation other that rational decision making and political calculation.

As the two leaders were agonizing over their decisions, the momentum of events continually threatened to take away their options. The Soviet buildup of troops and weapons continued. U.S. forces worldwide moved ahead with preparations for war. High- and low-level aerial reconnaissance over Cuba was stepped up. The tracking and pursuit of Soviet submarines intensified. Soviet ships continued steaming toward and through the quarantine zone. The leaders made threats against each other. It is impossible to count the things that could have gone wrong during the course of this conflict and especially during the four days of blockade. Both sides were in constant danger of losing control of any hostile incident that could have occurred between ships, submarines, aircraft, or even ground troops along the line at the Guantanamo Bay Naval Base.

The U-2 Crisis was exactly what everyone feared the most. This action by a Soviet commander in Cuba called for an automatic U.S. response. Interference with surveillance could not be tolerated. Kennedy had already been under intense pressure to use force to counter the uninterrupted Soviet buildup in Cuba. No one in the U.S. military or intelligence communities was happy with the prospect of a Soviet fortified stronghold in Cuba. The forces were assembled and ready to eliminate this threat. Before the missile crisis there had actually been discussion about manufacturing an incident to justify an invasion of Cuba.[188]

Since the beginning of the crisis, air strikes had been an attractive option. Here was immediate justification for that course, at least. If this incident had occurred a day earlier, retaliation would almost certainly have occurred, and, almost certainly, such retaliation would have been perceived in Cuba as the first phase of an invasion. Under these conditions local Soviet commanders would have been free to take whatever measures might have been necessary to defend themselves. Fearing a massive U.S. invasion, the Soviets held their tactical nuclear weapons at the ready. There is no evidence that U.S. military planners knew that these weapons were in Cuba or that the Soviets were prepared to use them if necessary.

It was not until 2004 that the U.S. military establishment learned that several Soviet submarines operating in Cuban waters during the crisis were armed with nuclear torpedoes. The antisubmarine task force that included the USS *Randolph* was considered an overwhelming force against isolated submarines. A nuclear weapon would have redressed this imbalance. The world never knew how close we came to a nuclear exchange at sea on Black Saturday.

Fortunately, by October 27, Khrushchev's offer of a settlement was on the table. Kennedy decided against the automatic response. He felt that he could live with the pressure for another day. Amazingly, this potential disaster turned out to be the critical ingredient in forcing all parties to the final settlement. McGeorge Bundy, Kennedy's national security advisor, later reflected on the U-2 incident and the death of Maj. Anderson: "In traditional terms he remained unavenged, but when we consider the role of his death in the decisions and communications that brought a rapid and decisive turn away from danger in less than one day's time, it becomes hard to think of any single sacrifice in the service of the United States that ever had larger consequences for good."[189] The U-2 Crisis was the climactic moment in an incredible sequence of events that occurred and potential disasters that didn't occur to enable the resolution of this crisis. Once again, the concept of good luck is strained by the concentration of so much of it.

In 1989 a conference was held in Moscow to review the Cuban Missile Crisis. It was attended by high-level officials from the U.S., U.S.S.R., and Cuba, who were directly involved, including Robert McNamara, McGeorge Bundy, Theodore Sorensen, Andrei Gromyko, and Anatoly Dobrynin. The conference report concluded that neither Kennedy nor Khrushchev ever had unfettered mastery of events during the crisis, and that further, the most grave dangers faced at the time were, "accidents, inadvertence, breakdowns of command and control, psychological pressures, and the limits of rationality under stress and uncertainty."[190] Other thought-provoking conclusions were made:

> "Sorenson sought to lay to rest the American perception, largely cultivated by earlier writings of his own, that the Cuban missile crisis was the Kennedy Administration's finest hour."

> "The extent to which all sides misjudged, misperceived, and misunderstood the actions and intentions of the other grows more astonishing with every new discovery."

> "The majority clearly concluded . . . that the risks of nuclear war had not only been greater than was previously thought but lay in dangers that had not been properly understood at the time."

I believe that these opinions formed by the principle advisors involved in the missile crisis support my view that God performed a miraculous work in bringing the world through this confrontation. Somehow, at the climactic moment, John Kennedy and Nikita Khrushchev found a way to step back from the inexorable pressure of events and to find within themselves the means to put aside political calculation and even self-interest. I believe that

God had a hand in providing that way. Finally, and significantly, one of the most striking features of the 1989 Moscow Conference was observed to be: "The extent to which participants on all sides have largely replaced self-congratulation with humility."[191] I believe that humility is the proper note on which to conclude this section. Anyone choosing to believe that an incredible sequence of brilliant decisions and good luck brought the world out of this crisis will probably not be convinced otherwise. I believe that a healthy sense of humility should lead anyone to at least wonder what role may have been played by God.

GOD'S PURPOSE

As we have seen, neither the United States nor the Soviet Union won the Cuban Missile Crisis. Both made significant sacrifices of their own aims to achieve an end to the confrontation. The Soviets had to live without a significant gain in strategic nuclear parity, and the United States had to live with Castro. To some extent, Cuba came out ahead with a guarantee that it would not be invaded, although it lost a major Soviet military presence in the bargain. As hands were removed from the trigger and military forces withdrawn, the winner was clearly mankind. I know of no other point in history when the world faced so much, if not total, destruction. All that can be said with certainty about God's purpose in bringing this crisis to an end is that the time had not yet arrived for the final chapter of history. This was not to be the day of Armageddon.

After the Cuban Missile Crisis, the Cold War continued for over twenty years. Although neither side won this long struggle, the self-destruction of the Soviet Union was complete by 1989, leaving America standing alone as the world's only superpower. Just as God brought America into existence and then shaped and protected her over the centuries, I believe that it was also his purpose to bring America through the struggle of the Cold War. Furthermore, I believe that it is reasonable to conclude that it was also his purpose that America should reach the point where it is today, in the preeminent position of power and influence on the world stage. I must admit that God's purpose at this point in history is less clear to me than in the earlier periods addressed in this book. Perhaps America is meant now to continue as an example to the world of what can be accomplished in a free society. Clearly, new levels of wealth and material progress are demonstrated every day. Spiritually, however, it is difficult to discern if America's example will prove to be positive or negative. Perhaps America is to be the place where the most ideal conditions of human freedom will permit the contest between good and evil to be played out and even finally resolved. For whatever ultimate purpose, I believe that God has brought America to this point in history and that he is waiting patiently to see the results.

So, if the Son sets you free, you will be free indeed.
—JOHN 8:36

CHAPTER SIX

THE HAND OF PROVIDENCE IN AMERICA'S WARS

DIVINE INTERVENTION

"To know the mind of God or his purposes is the most challenging interpretive activity in which a scholar could engage."[192] This quote from *In Defense of Miracles* is clearly true and, if anything, understates the difficulty of approaching this subject. Trying to understand how God may have intervened in history is definitely a challenging interpretive activity for anyone. Even so, religious writers have often and energetically engaged in this pursuit. The work cited above is a scholarly approach to the history and philosophical arguments for and against miracles. The authors postulate several levels of divine intervention short of the truly miraculous in which God acts through completely natural processes. A "miracle" is considered to be a direct act of God and must include some very unusual circumstances. Miracles can be either extraordinary events that temporarily violate natural laws or they can be a convergence of natural events in particularly unusual ways so as to produce amazing results.[193] Most of the incidents relating to America's wars described in this book would fall into the latter category.

In *Divine Interventions* Dan Millman and Doug Childers summarize centuries of evidence for God's hand in the lives of famous and obscure individuals from cultures around the world. They relate the story of Asoka, an ancient warrior king of an area now part of modern India. A spiritual vision came to Asoka causing him to forsake violence and to implement pacifist traditions that have affected Indian history for centuries.[194] Carl Jung's inner spiritual journey is recounted. The mystical and imaginary figure that he called Philemon is shown to have led Jung to revolutionary insights about the relationship between man's psychological and spiritual natures. The mysterious and miraculous transformation of Walt Whitman into a literary genius at age thirty-five is described.[195] Through fifty documented stories of a similar nature, divine forces are shown to have shaped history repeatedly. The works already cited by Peter Marshall and David Manuel focus more specifically on God's intervention in early American history and present their concept of God's plan and purpose for America and his influence over a broad spectrum of church and national life.

The Bible is of course the primary source of Jewish and Christian knowledge about God's intervention in the world. Growing up in the church, I always had a general knowledge of the familiar Bible stories which are full of God's heroes and miracles, such as Joshua at the Battle of Jericho, Jonah and the whale, Jesus feeding the five thousand, Paul's conversion on the road to Damascus, and many others. As a young skeptic, I was not content that all these wonderful things happened in the distant past, leaving me in the present with only old stories. Why would God have performed these miracles so long ago for others, leaving me to find my own faith in these accounts of old deeds? I always longed for something a little more direct from God and was disappointed when I never seemed to receive anything. As my skepticism grew over the years I intellectually discounted those biblical stories and other religious assertions about God's intervention in the world. I can easily understand how difficult it might be for skeptical readers to take seriously the conclusions I have drawn from the historical information presented in this book.

In *Miracles* Carol Neiman defines and describes miracles over the centuries and suggests that God's purpose in these acts is "to bring revelation—to grant us a glimpse of the divine, and, through that glimpse, the opportunity to be transformed." She also points out that often faith must come first, "to allow ourselves to go beyond our own self-imposed limitations and enter a realm where miracles are possible."[197] These apparently contradictory statements frame an important question. Can we be convinced of God's hand by evidence of it, or do we first have to have a faith that opens our eyes to the miraculous? It is obviously my hope that enough evidence can accomplish something toward transforming skeptical opinion. But I also know that it depends on how one looks at the evidence. In my own case it was a complicated process. A sense of the miraculous did lead me to Christ. On the other hand, my new faith opened my eyes to a new world of miracles. I know that an important personal change leading to my own conversion was the acquiring of a more childlike wonder toward the world around me. I began to appreciate more deeply many things in nature and in my own life, such as the beauty of a sunset, the radiance of a flower, the birth of my children, and the love of my wife. I began to see the miraculous nature of these everyday phenomena, and I began to sense God's presence in my life and in the world around me. I have tried to elaborate on this process in the Appendix by presenting my own Christian witness, hoping in the process to move skeptical readers even further toward serious consideration of how I interpret the historical "evidence" presented in this book.

I have used the phrases "hand of Providence," "God's hand," "divine intervention," "miracle," and "miraculous" almost interchangeably in referring to God's actions in history. These phrases, fortunately, lend themselves to broad interpretation. God has not been limited in his actions by our definitions or by our understanding or lack of understanding of his nature. I do believe that since biblical times God has rarely intervened in history in an overt way. Having given men and women the freedom to direct their own actions and to find their own beliefs, he has chosen normally not to intervene openly in their affairs. In *Tell Me Why* Michael Novak makes the point that:

> God ordinarily works through ordinary natural processes, not
> directly . . . the Creator of all things never relinquishes his sov-
> ereignty; he exercises it all the time, but only rarely by direct
> intervention.[198]

Most of the incidents described in this book are examples of God working through natural processes. We have seen many incidents which can be explained logically in isolation, but have produced extraordinary results at supremely critical moments. At such times it seems very feasible to differentiate between patterns of divine intervention and random luck.

AMERICA'S WARS

As I have become aware of miracles in nature and in my own life, it has become easier for me to consider the miraculous in history. We in fact don't have to go back to biblical times to see God's hand at work in the world. The focus of this book has been on much more recent times. On December 26, 1776, a mysterious attack lulled the Hessian garrison at Trenton into a false sense of security, leading to an incredible American victory. On September 13, 1862, a copy of Lee's orders were lost near Frederick, Maryland, leading directly to a complete change in the course of the Civil War. On June 4, 1942, engine trouble on a Japanese scout plane kept it from flying over the American fleet in time to give warning of an attack that would change the tide of World War II. Instead of triggering World War III, the destruction of an American U-2 reconnaissance aircraft on October 27, 1962, led directly to the resolution of the Cuban Missile Crisis. I believe that these and the other incidents described in this book are miraculous events that give strong evidence of God's hand at work in America's history.

It is my belief that God has also inspired men directly at times and given them insights or guided their actions toward what he wanted accomplished. At the climactic moment of the Cuban missile crisis, John Kennedy and Nikita Khrushchev both made decisions to give up goals to which each was committed, in the process risking their respective political futures. Since God has given men free will to make their own choices, it is difficult to discern when he is in control of such decisions. We never know what is in another's mind. In this case, however, I believe that there is such a miraculous outcome that God's hand can be seen in the actions of the principle participants. I believe that these decisions were part of a miraculous series of occurrences that brought the world back from the brink of destruction.

I know that my explanation of these events may not have proven God's presence in history. It does seem clear to me, however, that anyone, even a truly skeptical reader, has to see something at work beyond an incredible string of good luck. I point out again that I have not selected random events. These events have occurred at absolutely critical moments in America's past, when her survival was at stake. The climactic moments of the Revolutionary War, the Civil War, World War II, and the Cuban Missile Crisis were clearly in this category. If these events had taken a different turn, America might not exist today, at least in the form that we know it. These were of course not the only occasions when important issues were decided affecting America. The works of Peter Marshall and David Manuel have already been cited and are examples of efforts to show God's influence over a wider spectrum of America's history during the eighteenth and nineteenth centuries. Others already mentioned and many not mentioned have speculated on different aspects of God's influence on present and past events. However, the events presented in this book were crucial in a special way to the nation's birth and survival. I see a clear pattern of God's involvement in the history of America at these critical times.

GOD'S PURPOSE FOR AMERICA

I believe that freedom has been an important underlying theme in God's relationship with mankind and in his purpose for America. Christian belief holds that the most important event in history was Jesus Christ's coming into the world as a human being. However, even Jesus did not come as an all-powerful figure. Instead he took the form of a quiet spoken man and was often a servant to others. At the time most did not even understand who he was. In accordance with his own design, God has chosen rarely to overpower mankind with forceful demonstrations of his presence or his will. I think that it has never been in his plan for men to attempt the same thing. I believe that he has not looked favorably on the efforts of some men to control others, especially in spiritual matters. He has given men free will to live their own lives and to seek him or not. I believe that he has placed a need within every human being to turn to him, although this need is usually manifested in a very quiet voice. Each person must hear it for himself. There is no meaningful faith in God or relationship with him unless sought freely by each individual in response to that voice.

In modern history America has provided the model of this freedom to the world. I believe that it was God's purpose to bring this model into being and to nurture it for over two centuries. He has waited patiently to see the results and has at times intervened to guide his creation. Slavery was clearly not in accordance with his model of freedom. When political institutions failed to solve the incredibly complex problem of its unmaking, he allowed a bitter war to accomplish this purpose. For decades after the Civil War, America expanded across the continent and beyond, growing in stature among the nations of the world. Opposing Japanese expansion in the Far East, America found herself engaged in the Second World War, leading the fight for freedom in the world against Japan and Germany. I believe that it was God's purpose that America should defeat this aggression and emerge at a new level of power and influence. From this point America was confronted by the challenge of international Communism and a four-decade long worldwide struggle known as the Cold War. I believe that the totalitarian exercise of power and antipathy toward religious belief on the part of Communist governments was never in accordance with God's purpose. I believe that he brought both sides and the rest of the world through the dangers of the Cuban Missile Crisis in the climactic event of this long struggle. Communism would eventually be destroyed from within as America finally came to stand alone at the peak of power and influence in the world.

God has truly blessed America. The founding fathers had a God-given vision of how a free society should be structured. This structure has proven viable and stable throughout the nation's history, in contrast to chaotic conditions throughout much of the world. Americans have been free to develop the unlimited potential of the physical and intellectual resources provided them, in the process creating the most dynamic and wealthy society ever seen. Even though it has fallen short of its own promise on many occasions, America continues to be the land of opportunity and model of freedom to the world.

A by-product of America's freedom has been an economic well-being unprecedented in history. This freedom from want has, paradoxically, led to a materialism that often seems to crowd out God. When we consider the powerful tendency of the material world to supersede our spiritual lives, we begin to understand the significance of Jesus' words: "Blessed are the poor in spirit."[199] Material well-being, comfort, and overconfidence can certainly be stumbling blocks to the difficult process of introspection necessary to hear that quiet voice of God within. There is ample evidence that many in America are not hearing and are not trying to hear.

Statistically, the religious trends in America don't look good. Those classifying themselves Christian are projected to decline from 96 percent of the total population in 1900 to 85 percent in 2000. While the total of all other religious groups have shown a slight increase, those considered atheists and nonreligious have grown from 1.3 percent of the population to 9 percent. Also, many Christians have been counted only by census and are not associated with any church.[200] Of course these statistics don't reveal the truly faithful of any religion. That statistic is known only to God himself.

On a more positive note, it appears that those unaffiliated with a church have declined by about half as a percentage of total Christians.[201] Apparently there are fewer who are Christian in name only. With fewer attending churches on a perfunctory basis there is an opportunity to focus on more meaningful worship and spiritual growth. As faithful Christians have moved toward minority status within the culture, many have shown an increased resemblance to the earliest followers of Christ, fighting to survive spiritually and to carry his message to the world. There are many in need of this message. They continue to have the freedom to listen or to turn away, just as Christians continue to enjoy a large measure of freedom to encourage the choice in which they believe.

Americans have certainly exercised their freedom. From largely Christian beginnings a diverse society has evolved, incorporating every conceivable form of belief and unbelief. The Founding Fathers wisely ensured that there would be no established religion, in effect separating church and state. This has allowed every individual to freely pursue his own conscience in spiritual matters. This freedom has also been applied to a gradual purging of religious content from the affairs of government. Christian traditions have been challenged wherever they have appeared in public institutions and ceremonies. There has often been more public support for atheism than for Christianity or any other organized religion. I give no credit to those leading the fight against religion in our public institutions; however, I believe that this is not the issue that concerns God. He is concerned with what every individual does with the freedom given him or her. Our individual response to God is what is critical to God.

FREEDOM IN CHRIST

The concept of responding to God is one that many, if not most, find difficult to grasp. Human nature and human institutions have presented almost insurmountable obstacles to this process. The free will that God has given mankind permits a focus on immediate and physical needs, often at the expense of long-term and spiritual needs. Many do not even consider the possibility of an ultimate or eternal need. Every single human being causes harm or disappointment to others at various times. The injury is often in the failure to take an appropriate action. Mankind has always been plagued with thoughtless and destructive behaviors. Governments, social organizations, and religions have evolved focusing on these behaviors and attempting to ameliorate them. Rules, laws, moral codes, and commandments have proliferated with elaborate systems of intrinsic and extrinsic rewards and punishments. Who could satisfy every demand? The criminal and immoral mostly don't care. The good often do their best and still face the guilt associated with failing to meet every expectation. The good and the bad, to various degrees, are all subject to that guilt and the anxieties associated with it. Mankind was given free will and a deep-seated need for God, but not perfection. We in fact seem to be prisoners of our imperfection.

Christians believe that God provided the solution to this condition over two thousand years ago. To demonstrate his love for humanity he sent his Son, in essence himself, into the world. Jesus came to destroy the barriers separating men and women from God. He brought a simple message of forgiveness and reconciliation. Through Jesus every human being was given a clear and direct way to God. He prayed, "Righteous Father, I have made you known to them . . . in order that the love you have for me may be in them."[202] The appropriate response to God is simply to accept this gift. I bear witness to the amazing truth that this simple act opens new doors to a spiritual life in relationship with God. The ultimate freedom comes from such a relationship and the knowledge that this relationship can exist in this lifetime and in the eternal future. "You will know the truth and the truth will set you free."[203] "If the Son sets you free, you will be free indeed."[204]

TOWARD THE FUTURE

It would be presumptuous on my part to speculate about how God now views America or any other part of his creation. However, I do believe that his hand has been active in guiding America to the point where it is today. We see a society blessed with a degree of freedom from political tyranny and physical deprivation unparalleled in history. Never have more people had the opportunity and complete freedom to consider for themselves the meaning of their own lives and of life itself, and the freedom to turn to or away from God. Although he leaves each to make his own choice, I believe that he wants every individual to freely decide to come to him. We are told that, "He is patient with you, not wanting anyone to perish."[205] With his great commission Jesus challenged his faithful to "go and make disciples of all nations."[206] I believe that a benevolent God expects his faithful to pursue their mission and that he waits to see how each individual will respond to his continuing call.

Of course no one knows how long he will wait. Christians do believe in a day of final judgment and an end to the world as it now exists. This subject seems to command the attention of many in our society today. The *Left Behind* series of books by Tim LaHaye and Jerry Jenkins has dominated best-seller lists for several years, and bookstore shelves are crowded with other titles related to the end times. Jesus himself spoke about his eventual return. His disciples asked him when, and he told them, "Just as it was in the days of Noah, so it will be in the days of the Son of Man."[207] The "days of Noah" refer to the ancient time of the Old Testament Flood. At that time, we read that, "The Lord saw how great man's wickedness on the earth had become."[208] God apparently concluded that there was then no hope for the mass of humanity, and he therefore brought destruction to the world. On a smaller scale, he destroyed Sodom when he was finally unable to find even ten righteous people living there. From this biblical perspective we might conclude that God could even now be weighing mankind's condition. Perhaps he is gauging the effectiveness of Christians in carrying out Jesus' great commission. Perhaps he waits to see what direction mankind will take as he provides conditions of greater freedom for the exercise of the free will that he has given every individual. Maybe he waits for evidence of a final, irreversible trend either way.

After the Flood, God gave mankind a new beginning. Centuries later Jesus Christ brought another new beginning to a world unable to find God through the religious practices of the time. In modern times I believe that America has in some sense also been a new beginning. In this case we see a new beginning in political and social conditions, where governmental and religious structures were removed which attempted to compel citizens toward a forced religious conformity. Many who are religious themselves often see our present state as deplorable due to the bad choices that they perceive many to be making. However, I believe that this is the condition that God has intended. These choices must be freely made. Christians believe that God created mankind to share and even understand in a limited way his love. For this to be possible, men and women need the free will to make their own choices. Unfortunately, this freedom also allows the choice of evil. I believe that God's hand has been involved in bringing us to the time and situation where we have those choices, and that he is waiting to see the outcome. I also believe that we are on a timetable that only he understands.

In addressing the subject of God's purpose in America's history, I have tried to be conscious of my limitations. As it is written:

The wisdom of the wise will perish.[209] Where is the wise man? Where is the scholar? Where is the philosopher of this age? Has not God made foolish the wisdom of the world?[210]

So, I bring great humility to the task of presenting my own wisdom. My ideas have come from intensive study and thought, but have also involved much prayerful speculation on my part. It is my belief that there is abundant evidence showing that God has been intimately involved in history and has had a special purpose for America. If this is true, many unanswered questions still remain. How does God look at America now? Is America moving in the right direction? Will America continue to occupy this special place? Are God's faithful doing enough? How long will God wait? Since these questions can't be answered, and we can't know God's plans for the future, we are left only with the choices of the present. And these are individual choices. Every individual continues to face his or her own spiritual journey, drawing nearer to God or moving further away. Christians have a special opportunity and responsibility to share the gift they profess to have received. God continues to reach out and to give us time and the freedom to choose. How the free will that we have as individuals and as a nation intersects with God's plans is a mystery known only to him. His ultimate purpose for America and his final judgment of each American's response will be revealed at the time that he chooses. I fear that many will be found lacking when that time comes. It is my prayer that the religious skeptics who read this book will be persuaded by the evidence to acknowledge God's hand in history and in their own lives. I pray that this is their first step toward accepting the gift offered by God's Son: the ultimate freedom found only in a personal relationship with God.

And there was war in heaven.

—REVELATION 12:7

WAR ON FREEDOM

A T 8:45 A.M. *on September 11, 2001, an American Airlines Boeing 767 was flown into the north tower of the World Trade Center by a group of religious zealots. A new war was declared on America. This attack was quickly followed by others as the world watched in dismay. The hijackers had labored patiently and in obscurity for years for this one act, which they knew they would not survive. The objective was simple: To inflict pain on America. Untold pain was indeed the result. President George W. Bush asserted then that the United States had become engaged in the first war of the twenty-first century.*

HOW COULD GOD ALLOW THIS TO HAPPEN?

As I watched the sad and frustrating aftermath of these events, I prayed as never before for God's blessing on America and the rest of the free world. It was obvious then that this would not be an easy war. The road has indeed been long and difficult, and many wounds are yet to be suffered and inflicted.

One of my most disturbing images from the disaster of September 11th was an injured victim asking, "How could God allow this to happen?" I feel the need to respond to this cry in the most emphatic terms. God did not cause this tragedy. Men and women perpetrated these events. They were following, and others will continue to follow, the logic of a cause foreign to our deepest understanding of right and wrong.

EVIL

This book has focused on America's past wars and her enemies in those wars. America has fought against England, Japan, Germany, and the Soviet Union. She has also fought a great internal war. The recurring theme of these conflicts has been freedom. America has stood for this cause throughout her history. I have tried to be fair throughout this book in showing the factors motivating America's opponents in these events.

Up until now I have been very sparing in the use of the word *evil*. In our modern world this term is considered by many to be obsolete. Few are comfortable with labeling anyone or anything as evil. The lament of our age is, "Who are we to judge?" I have already confessed my lack of theological expertise to address this subject, and I again reassert that fact. I believe that there is evil in the world, but I am not able to explain it completely.

Confronted with the incredible nature of terrorist attacks on unsuspecting and defenseless people, I consider theological argument to be largely irrelevant. We must simply face the fact that evil exists. People do things that are unthinking, unjust, and cruel. Sometimes there are underlying causes, and sometimes there are not. Sometimes evil shows itself in small actions and attitudes. Sometimes it is monstrous.

I will leave it to others to assert whether this evil is a coherent force in the world orchestrated by a malevolent and satanic power, or whether it is the simple distorted exercise of individual free will. The results are the same. The events of September 11, 2001, seem to me to argue for the more expansive view of a larger force at work. It is hard to believe that such diabolical acts could originate in human minds.

GOD'S PURPOSE

In this book I have tried to show how God has worked in history to accomplish his purposes. It has been my perception that freedom has been an underlying theme. I have tried to carefully show how difficult it would have been on many occasions to know what that purpose was at the time that events were happening. I reassert that caution now. We can only pray and sincerely seek discernment about what God might be seeking to accomplish in the world at this time.

I concluded Chapter Six by stating my belief that God has perfected the conditions of freedom in America for a purpose. He has created these conditions to allow the fullest exercise of the free will that he has given mankind. Only when individuals are free is faith meaningful in God's sight. I believe that, above all else, he waits for individual men and women to seek that faith and a relationship with him. He wants every individual to come to him, but knows, by the nature of his creation, that all will not. He waits to see.

Where does America stand now with God? Only God knows the answer. He has blessed America lavishly throughout her history. As America has grown in power and influence in the world, her example to the world has grown in importance and scope. Economically, she continues to be a light to the world. The question remains, what does America stand for spiritually? I am not alluding to an official position or advocacy of Christianity or another religion. Where do her individual citizens stand spiritually? Are they satisfied, or are they seeking? What are they seeking? What are they doing with the freedoms that a very few have earned and most have inherited? God is waiting to see.

On September 11, 2001, war was declared on freedom itself in America and in the world. It is a matter of my own faith that this evil will not prevail. God's love and his kingdom on earth will prevail. Our problem is that we don't know when this will happen. We can only pray that God continues to bless and to have a purpose for America. Whether that proves to be true or not may lie in the hands and hearts of Americans themselves. God did not cause this act of war. However, he may use this disaster as another test, or even as a final exam, for America.

A NEW WAR

As a Christian and as a military man, I long to see America's patriotic spirit of old renewed as a new generation lays claim to the title, "Greatest." I long to see this new evil humbled and humiliated before the world. Unfortunately, God's victory may come in a way and at a time that we won't see or understand. I must simply pray that God will continue to bless America and enable her to rise to these challenges. I pray that America proves herself worthy.

In fighting this new war, we need to understand that all must be soldiers in it. There can be no conscientious objectors or draft dodgers. No one stays home while the "boys" go off to fight. The fight has already come here, and every citizen shares the danger. The heroes of September 11th were policemen and firemen. Today they are soldiers and Marines and countless citizens who wear no uniform at all.

The ultimate target of our enemies is not our buildings or even our lives. The ultimate target is our freedom. Our enemies will try to create fear and hate. If they are successful, our minds and spirits will be captured by their evil. In its purest form this is a spiritual war. Americans must go back to their spiritual roots and reaffirm the purpose of their own freedoms. They must use their freedoms foremost to pursue their own understanding and relationship to God. Only in God will we find the strength and perseverance to prevail. Only as God's children will we deserve to prevail.

America! America!
God mend thine every flaw,
Confirm thy soul in self-control
Thy liberty in law.

—"AMERICA THE BEAUTIFUL"
BY KATHERINE LEE BATES

WAR AND GOD
IN MY OWN LIFE

W AR HAS BEEN an important part of my family history. My ancestors fought in the Civil War, and I can hardly remember not knowing about Robert E. Lee, Stonewall Jackson, Jeb Stuart, and other great Southern leaders. Their skill, daring, and devotion to duty in support of a heroic but lost cause stirred my imagination as a boy. The concept of the officer as a gentleman and a warrior shaped my life and especially my career as a Marine Corps officer. My grandfather served as a medical officer in France during World War I. My father was commissioned in the navy during World War II. He commanded naval detachments on merchant vessels convoying across the North Atlantic during the height of the German U-boat crisis. My twin uncles joined the Army Air Corps and flew together as pilot and copilot in a twin-engine B-26 bomber. They died together when shot down over Holland in 1943. My older brothers were air force pilots and one flew F-84 "thunderjets" during the Korean War, specializing in low-level bombing and close air support. To complete this family picture I saw combat duty as a marine rifle company commander in Vietnam. My mother once made the observation that she had sent men to every war of this century, including her father, her brothers, her husband, and two sons.

One aspect of my family's military background has been its association with The Citadel, the Military College of South Carolina. My sons graduated in 1998 and 2007, completing the fourth generation of direct father-son line. I graduated in 1961, the year of the centennial celebration of the beginning of the Civil War. The Corps of Cadets staged a reenactment of Citadel cadets firing the first shots of the war on the federal ship *Star of the West* attempting to resupply Fort Sumter. I was well schooled in the history of that conflict. I completed my final tour of duty as a marine officer at The Citadel as a professor of Naval Science and Tactical Officer to the Corps of Cadets. Among other subjects I taught courses in modern amphibious warfare, spanning the Gallipoli campaign in World War I, the European and Pacific theaters of World War II, the Inchon landings in Korea, and the Deckhouse Operations of Vietnam. During this time I had the opportunity to research the historical roots of many of the techniques and methods that I had practiced with amphibious units in the field.

War was my profession throughout my career as a marine officer. I studied military history, tactics and strategy continuously. Over the course of my career I attended the Marine Officer Basic School, U.S. Army Ranger, Airborne, and Special Forces Officer Schools, and the Canadian Forces Command and Staff College. I was constantly challenged to learn lessons in tactics and strategy appropriate to my level of rank and higher, and to incorporate these lessons into my actions as an infantry commander and staff officer. Military history was far more than an academic pursuit. The lessons learned pertained directly to my professional effectiveness.

I present this discourse on my personal and family background to explain my interest in military matters and to point out that I have utilized my own professional background and general understanding of war and military history in preparing the historical aspects of this work. With limited expertise as a historian, I have of necessity followed a commonsense approach to research and have tried to ensure that every historical point is fully documented. I have often successfully located the true source documents pertaining to events covered. I have also often relied on and benefited from the research of others.

My interest in God has been continuing and at times intense throughout my life, especially in recent years since becoming a Christian. To some extent this interest flows also from my ancestry that includes a Presbyterian minister great-grandfather and a family tree full of devout churchgoers. I was raised in a small town Presbyterian Church and learned my catechism at an early age. As I got older and experienced difficulty understanding the God portrayed by my Sunday school teachers, I gradually distanced myself from the organized religion of the church. As I entered college and began my professional life in the Marine Corps, I began to pursue my questions about God in literature, poetry, philosophy, and science. This pursuit has gone on all my life, mostly outside, occasionally inside the church.

As a young person I tried to pray, although unfortunately I never received much satisfaction from the effort. I never had much sense of progress in communicating with God or in establishing a relationship with him. At about age twenty-one I went through an intense period of prayer and meditation seeking some sign or communication from God at what I thought was a critical juncture of my life. This ended in frustration when I seemed to hear nothing. At the time I concluded that God did not intend that I should understand him. He would continue to be a remote

Being with no direct connection to my life. At this point I had the Golden Rule and my duty as a Marine Corps officer. These were enough for a meaningful life at that time.

During my career in the Marine Corps, I turned to God occasionally, usually during moments of crisis. The incident described in Chapter One is an example. Fearing for my life and with little else on my mind, I did do some intense praying. I wasn't conscious at the time of being heard, and I don't recall giving God much credit for the outcome. Usually I was too focused on the business at hand to think much about spiritual matters.

For the most part my experiences in combat seemed to have little connection with God. A marine infantry unit is trained and intended to be tough, aggressive, and violent. Marines learn the importance of esprit de corps, which is an almost religious belief in themselves and each other. Everything else is generally regarded with some degree of irreverence. I can't speak for others, but I know that I never thought much about God. I was often scared, frustrated, and angry. I saw a lot of suffering and death and felt that these came too randomly. I had the feeling of using up a certain amount of luck every day, as if I had been allotted a finite amount of it. It was hard then to see God's hand in much of this. There was mainly the day-to-day struggle to get the job done and to survive. As I reflect back, I do now recall the selflessness of many young marines and navy corpsmen who helped each other in tough times, often heroically. There was a bond of trust and affection between fellow marines that sustained us all through everything. At the time I didn't see God in any of these things, obviously due to the fact that I wasn't looking.

Considering the Vietnam War in general, I have always believed that our cause was right. America's purpose was to nurture freedom in that country by opposing a Communist takeover.

For better or worse we limited ourselves to a defensive war. The aggression that we faced there was not as overt as in previous wars and the roots of the conflict were complex. To some extent the North Vietnamese aims were nationalistic as well as Communistic. The question remains as to whether the Vietnam War had more to do with America's worldwide confrontation with Communism or with an internal struggle to reunify that country. I believe that both aspects were involved and could not be separated. When that reunification did finally take place, it was more than an internal matter. Communism gained ground in Vietnam, Laos, and Cambodia. The light of freedom was dimmed in the process. The silver lining to this frustrating struggle may have been that other countries were saved from facing Communist insurgencies during those years and after. I believe that God was with America during the long years of the Cold War, and I would especially like to believe that God approved of her effort to give freedom a chance in South Vietnam.

My conversion to Christianity came at age fifty-three as the culmination of a long process. I apparently had to reach that age and point in life to finally realize that I was not in control of everything in my life. Grown and growing children clearly brought this fact to light. It also slowly dawned on me that I would probably never be able to fully live up to the duties and obligations which I had always set for myself. I had always considered myself to be basically a good person, but I became more aware over the years of things that I did or didn't do that were disappointing to myself and to others. Even though I had maintained an active interest in God and religion for most of my life, God remained an abstraction. I came to a point where I had to admit to myself that I in fact had a spiritual void within myself. I also had to admit that I was unable to fill this void through my own intellectual effort. I owe these insights to my experiences within the Episcopal Church and to one of its spiritual renewal programs called Cursillo.

At this point I was blessed with the opportunity to meet and to hear General Charles Duke tell about the spiritual changes in his life. As a former astronaut and military man his words spoke to me in a particularly meaningful way. He said that he finally came to realize that it is impossible to view Jesus Christ as simply a great teacher or historical figure if we look carefully at what he said. He is either what he claimed to be, the Son of God, or the biggest fraud in history. We are faced with a question. We can read, study, think, and weigh the pros and cons. However, we can't weigh the pros and cons forever. At some point, we have to decide our own answer to that question. *Decide* was apparently the word that God meant for me to hear. Making a decision was a process that I understood and could do when necessary. I decided on that day to accept Jesus for what he claimed to be and to ask him to be a part of my life. A conscious part of this decision was a suspension of many skeptical attitudes that had always prevented any spiritual event from occurring in my life. I decided to take this small step and to see what would happen.

Although this was the most significant event of my life, I did not experience any sudden revelation or blinding light. I did have the experience of beginning to move in a new direction. In retrospect I began a slow process of spiritual awakening. I became intensely interested in Scripture and found more and more of it relevant to myself. I began seeking more knowledge about God as I pursued a relationship with him through prayer, study, and an effort to lead a Christian life. This has led to a slow and unsteady process of spiritual growth. Although the process has been slow, a new sense of God soon became apparent. Instead of an abstraction, he became a reality in my life in a personal way. I found it very natural to pray and to listen. I have learned to work at discerning his answers and sensing his presence in my life. I have come to a strong belief that he has been involved in my life and has blessed my life, even when I was not aware of him. Even though he has always been there, he has given me the freedom to find my own direction. As I have considered my own life and pursued my interests in history, I have become convinced that God has worked in the lives of men and women throughout time. He made the world for human beings and gave them freedom to make their own choices. At times he intervenes in their affairs, although usually in ways that require an effort to discern. This realization has inspired my effort in writing this book.

BIBLIOGRAPHY

CHAPTER ONE—INTRODUCTION

Askew, Thomas A. and Peter W. Spellman, *The Churches and the American Experience*. Michigan: Baker Book House, 1984.

Booty, John E. *The Church in History*. New York: The Seabury Press, 1979.

Cragg, G. R. *The Church and the Age of Reason* 1648–1789. Middlesex, England: Pelican Books, 1960.

Einstein, Albert. *Out of My Later Years*. New York: Bonanza Books, 1956.

Ferris, Timothy. *Coming of Age in the Milky Way*. New York: Anchor Books, 1988.

Friedman, Milton and Rose Friedman. *Free to Choose, A Personal Statement*. New York and London: Harcourt Brace Jovanovich, 1980.

Gould, Stephen Jay. *Eight Little Piggies. Reflections in Natural History*. New York and London: W. W. Norton & Company, 1993.

Hudson, Winthrop S. and John Corrigan. *Religion in America*, 6th ed. Upper Saddle River, NJ: Prentice Hall, 1999.

Kushner, Harold S. *When Bad Things Happen to Good People*. New York: Avon Books, 1981.

Lucas, Laddie. *Out of the Blue. The Role of Luck in Air Warfare, 1917–1966*. London: Hutchinson, 1985.

McCallum, Martha and Jane Hamblin. *God's Incredible Plan*. Old Tappan, NJ: Fleming H. Revell Co., 1978.

Montross, Lynn, *War Through the Ages*. 3rd ed. New York: Harper and Brothers Publishers, 1960.

Perry, Marvin. *A History of the World*. Boston: Houghton Mifflin Company, 1985.

Preston, Richard A., Sydney F. Wise and Harmon O. Werner. *Men in Arms. A History of Warfare and its Interrelationships with Western Society*, rev. ed. New York: Frederick A. Praeger, 1962.

Shepherd, William R. *Shepherd's Historical Altas*. 9th ed. New York: Barnes & Noble Books, 1964.

Vagts, Alfred. *A History of Militarism, Civilian and Military*. London: Hollis & Carter, 1959.

Wells, H. G. *The Outline of History*. rev. New York: Garden City of Books, 1961.

CHAPTER TWO—AMERICAN REVOLUTION

Bobrick, Benson. *Angel in the Whirlwind, The Triumph of the American Revolution*. New York: Simon & Schuster, 1997.

Chidsey, Donald Barr. *The Tide Turns, An Informal History of the Campaign of 1776 in the American Revolution*. New York: Crown Publishers, Inc., 1966.

Churchill, Winston S. *The Age of Revolution, of A History of the English-Speaking Peoples*. New York: Dodd, Mead & Company, 1967.

Cook, Don. *The Long Fuse. How England Lost the American Colonies, 1760–1785*. New York: The Atlantic Monthly, 1975.

Durant, Will. *The Reformation, 1300–1564*, Vol. VI of *The Story of Civilization*. New York: Simon and Schuster, 1957.

Durant, Will and Ariel. *The Age of Voltaire, 1715–1756*, Vol. IX of *The Story of Civilization*. New York: Simon and Schuster, 1965.

Durant, Will and Ariel. *Rousseau and Revolution, 1715-1787*, Vol. X of *The Story of Civilization*. New York: Simon and Schuster, 1967.

Dwyer, William M. *The Day is Ours! November 1776–January 1777: An Inside View of the Battles of Trenton and Princeton*. New York: The Viking Press, 1983.

Fast, Howard. *The Crossing*. New York: William Morrow and Company, Inc., 1971.

Fleming, Thomas. *1776, Year of Illusions*. New York: W. W. Norton Company, Inc., 1975.

Henderson, Peter. *Campaign of Chaos...1776*. Haworth, NJ: Archives Ink, Ltd., 1975.

Irving, Washington. *George Washington, A Biography*. New York: Da Capo Press, 1994.

Johnson, Curt. *Battles of the American Revolution*. New York: Rand McNally & Company, 1975.

Lancaster, Bruce. *From Lexington to Liberty, The Story of the American Revolution*. Garden City, NY: Doubleday & Company, Inc., 1955.

Madaras, Larry and James M. SoRelle, eds. *The Colonial Period to Reconstruction*. Vol. I of *Taking Sides, Clashing Views on Controversial Issues in American History*. The Dushkin Publishing Group, Inc., 1989.

Marshall, Peter and David Manuel. *The Light and the Glory*. Old Tappan, NJ: Fleming H. Revell Company, 1977.

Middlekauff, Robert. *The Glorious Cause, The American Revolution 1763–1789*. New York: Oxford University Press, 1982.

Morgan, Kenneth O., ed. *The Oxford History of Britain*. Oxford: Oxford University Press, 1988.

Reid, Stuart and Paul Chappell. *King George's Army 1740–1793* of the Men-at-Arms Series. London: Reed International Books Ltd., 1995.

Stember, Sol. *The Bicentennial Guide to the American Revolution*. New York: Saturday Review Press, 1974.

Stryker, William S. *The Battles of Trenton and Princeton.* Boston and New York: Houghton, Mifflin and Company, The Riverside Press, 1898. Spartanburg, SC: The Reprint Company, 1967.

Symonds, Craig L. *A Battlefield Atlas of the American Revolution.* Baltimore, MD: The Nautical and Aviation Publishing Co. of America, 1986.

Thayer, William Roscoe. *George Washington.* Boston and New York: Houghton Mifflin Company, 1922.

Wallace, Willard M. *Appeal to Arms, A Military History of the American Revolution.* Chicago: Quadrangle Books, 1951.

Wood, W. J. *Battles of the Revolutionary War 1775-1781.* Chapel Hill, NC: Algonquin Books, 1990.

Zlatich, Marko and Peter F. Copeland. *General Washington's Army 1775–1778.* Men-at-Arms Series. London: Osprey Publishing Ltd., 1994.

CHAPTER 3—CIVIL WAR

Bailey, Ronald H. *The Civil War, The Bloodiest Day.* Alexandria, VA: Time-Life Books, 1984.

Basler, Roy P. *A Short History of the American Civil War.* New York: Basic Books, Inc. 1967.

Catton, Bruce. "Crisis at the Antietam," in *The Civil War.* Ed. Stephen W. Sears, Boston: Houghton Mifflin Company, 1991.

Chase, Salmon. "Emancipation," in *The Lincoln Reader.* Ed. Paul M. Angle, New Brunswick: Rutgers University Press, 1947.

Connelly, Thomas L. andBarbara L. Bellows. *God and General Longstreet, The Lost Cause and the Southern Mind.* Baton Rouge and London: Louisiana State University Press, 1982.

Crook, D. P. *Diplomacy During the American Civil War.* New York: JohnWiley and Son, Inc., 1975.

Current, Richard N. *The Lincoln Nobody Knows.* New York: Hill and Wang, 1958.

Donald, David Herbert. *Lincoln.* New York: Simon & Schuster, 1995.

Eaton, Clement. *Jefferson Davis.* New York: The Free Press, 1977.

Freeman, Douglas Southall. *Lee's Lieutenants, A Study in Command.* 3 vols. New York: Charles Scribner's Sons 1942–1944.

Johnson, Robert Underwood and Clarence Clough Buel, eds. *Battles and Leaders of the Civil War.* New York: The Century Co., 1884, 1887, 1988.

Ketchum, Richard M., ed. *The American Heritage Picture History of the Civil War.* Narrated by Bruce Catton. New York: American Heritage, 1960.

Lee, Robert E. *The Story of Robert E. Lee, As Told in His Own Words.* Edited by Ralston B. Lattimore. Philadelphia: Eastern National Park & Monument Assoc., 1964.

Lincoln, Abraham. *The Collected Works of Abraham Lincoln.* Vols. I–VIII, Roy P. Basler, ed. New Brunswick, NJ: Rutgers University Press, 1953.

Marshall, Peter, and David Manuel. *Sounding Forth the Trumpet.* Grand Rapids, MI: Fleming H. Revell, 1997.

McCake, James B. Jr. *Life and Campaigns of General Robert E. Lee.* Atlanta: National Publishing Co., 1866.

McClellan, George B. *The Civil War Papers of George B. McClellan, Selected Correspondence 1860–1865.* Edited by Stephen W. Sears. New York: Ticknor & Fields, 1989.

Oates, Stephen B. *With Malice Toward None, A Life of Abraham Lincoln.* New York: Harper Perannial, 1997.

Priest, John Michael. *Before Antietam: The Battle for South Mountain.* New York: Oxford University Press, 1992.

Shaara, Jeff. *Gods and Generals.* New York: Ballantine Books, 1996.

Welles, Gideon. *Civil War and Reconstruction.* Ed. Albert Mordell. New York: Twayne Publishers, 1959.

CHAPTER 4—WORLD WAR II

Allen, Thomas B. "Return to the Battle of Midway," *National Geographic,* Vol. 195, No. 4, April, 1999, pp. 80–103.

Barker, A. J. *Midway: The Turning Point*. New York: Ballantine Books Inc., 1971.

Bocking, Brian. *A Popular Dictionary of Shinto*. Chicago: NTC Publishing Group, 1951.

Busch, Noel F. *The Horizon Concise History of Japan*. New York: American Heritage Publishing Co., 1972.

Durant, Will. *Our Oriental Heritage*. Vol. I of *The Story of Civilization*. New York: Simon and Schuster, 1954.

Editors of Time-Life Books. *Japan at War*. Alexandria, VA: Time-Life Books, 1980.

Farris, Marvin. *Do It Again . . . Was It Luck or Prayer?* Fort Worth, TX: Branch-Smith, Inc., c. 1969.

Fuchida, Mitsuo and Masatake Okumiya. *Midway: The Battle That Doomed Japan*. Annapolis, MD: U.S. Naval Institute, 1955.

Hart, Robert A. *The Eccentric Tradition. American Diplomacy in the Far East*. New York: Charles Scribner's Sons, 1976.

Leonard, Jonathan Norton. *Early Japan*. New York: Time-Life Books, 1968.

Leverton, J. Wilson Jr., Rear Admiral. *Recollections of Fleet Admiral Chester W. Nimitz*, Interviewed by Dr. John T. Mason Jr., Aug. 22, 1969, Naval Historical Collection, Naval War College, Newport, RI.

Macksey, Kenneth. *Military Errors of World War Two*. London: Cassell, 1987.

Mitchell, Lt. Col. Joseph B. and Sir Edward S. Creasy. *Twenty Decisive Battles of the World*. New York: The Macmillan Company, 1964.

Morison, Samuel Eliot. *The Two-Ocean War. A Short History of the United States Navy in the Second World War*. Boston and Toronto: Little, Brown and Company, 1963.

Neumann, William L. *America Encounters Japan. From Perry to MacAuthur*. Baltimore: The Johns Hopkins Press, 1963.

Office of Naval Intelligence. *The Japanese Story of the Battle of Midway*. U.S. Navy, 1947.

Potter, E. B. and Chester W. Nimitz. *Sea Power, A Naval History*. Englewood Cliffs, NJ: Prentice-Hall, Inc., 1960.

Reischauer, Edwin O. *The United States and Japan.* Cambridge, MA.: Harvard University Press, 1965.

Simons, Gerald, ed. *Japan at War.* Alexandria, VA: Time-Life Books, 1980.

Spector, Ronald H. *Eagle Against the Sun. The American War with Japan.* New York: The Free Press, 1985.

Taylor, Theodore. *The Battle Off Midway Island.* New York: Avon Books, 1981.

CHAPTER FIVE—COLD WAR

Allison, Graham T. Jr. "Introduction," *The Secret Cuban Missile Crisis Documents.* Washington: Brassey's (US), 1994.

Beer, Robert M. *The U. S. Navy and the Cuban Missile Crisis.* Annapolis, MD: U.S. Naval Academy, 1990.

Blight, James G. and David A. Welch. *On the Brink. Americans and Soviets Reexamine the Cuban Missile Crisis.* New York: The Noonday Press, 1990.

Boiter, Albert. *Religion in the Soviet Union.* The Center for Strategic and International Studies, Georgetown University. Beverly Hill/London: Sage Publications, 1980.

Bundy, McGeorge. *Danger and Survival, Choices About the Bomb in the First Fifty Years.* New York: Random House, 1988.

Central Intelligence Agency. *The Secret Cuban Missile Crisis Documents.* Washington: Brassey's (US), 1994.

Errickson, Jon Andrew. *The Cuban Missile Crisis of 1962: Miscalculations, Escalation, and Near Nuclear Confrontation.* Florida State University, 1994.

Fursenko, Aleksander and Timothy Naftali. *"One Hell of a Gamble." Krushchev, Castro, and Kennedy, 1958–1964.* New York and London: W. W. Norton & Company, 1997.

Gribkov, General Anatoli I. and General William Y. Smith. *Operation Anadyr, U. S. and Soviet Generals Recount the Cuban Missile Crisis.* Chicago, Berlin, Tokyo, and Moscow: edition q, inc., 1994.

Halberstam, David. *The Fifties.* New York: Villard Books, 1993.

Hersh, Seymour M. *The Dark Side of Camilot.* Boston, New York, Toronto, London: Little, Brown and Company, 1997.

Hosking, Geoffrey. *The First Socialist Society. A History of the Soviet Union from Within,* Second Enlarged Edition. Cambridge, MA: Harvard University Press, 1992.

Kennedy, Robert F. *Thirteen Days, A Memoir of the Cuban Missile Crisis.* New York: Mentor, 1969.

Khrushchev, Nikita. *Khrushchev Remembers.* Trans. and ed. by Strobe Talbott, Boston and Toronto: Little, Brown and Company, 1970.

Khruschev, Nikita. *Khruschev Remembers. The Glasnost Tapes.* Trans. and ed. by Jerrold L. Schecter. Boston, Toronto, and London: Little, Brown and Company, 1990.

Love, Robert W. Jr. *History of the U. S. Navy, 1942–1991.* Harrisburg, PA: Stackpole Books, 1992.

Naval History Division. *American Naval Fighting Ships.* Vol. VI. Washington: Department of the Navy, 1976.

Parsons, Howard L. *Christianity Today in the USSR.* New York: International Publishers, 1987.

Penkovskiy, Oleg. *The Penkovskiy Papers.* New York: Doubleday & Company, Inc., 1965.

Perez-Stable, Marifili. *The Cuban Revolution. Origins, Course, Legacy,* 2nd. ed. New York and Oxford: Oxford University Press, 1999.

Revelations from the Russian Archives, Documents in English Translation. Ed. Diane P. Koenker and Ronald D. Bachman. Washington, DC: Library of Congress, 1997.

Rhodes, Richard. *The Making of the Atomic Bomb.* New York: Simon and Schuster, 1986.

Szasz, Fernenc M. *The Day the Sun Rose Twice, The Story of the Trinity Site Nuclear Explosion, July 16, 1945.* Albuquerque: University of New Mexico Press, 1984.

Tompson, William J. *Khrushchev. A Political Life.* New York: St. Martin's Griffin, 1997.

CHAPTER SIX—THE HAND OF PROVIDENCE
IN AMERICA'S WARS

Britannica Book of the Year, 1999. Encyclopaedia Britannica, Inc., 1999.

Geivett, R. Douglas andGary R. Habermas, ed. *In Defense of Miracles, A Comprehensive Case for God's Action in History.* Downers Grove, IL: InterVarsity Press, 1997.

Millman, Dan and Doug Childers. *Divine Interventions, True Stories of Mystery and Miracles that Change Lives.* Emmaus, PA: Daybreak Books/Rodale Books, 1999.

Neiman, Carol. *Miracles, The Extraordinary, the Impossible, and the Divine.* New York: Viking Studio Books, 1995.

Novak, Michael and Jana Novak. *Tell Me Why.* New York: Pocket Books, 1998.

U.S. Bureau of the Census. *Statistical Abstract of the United States: 1998* (118th Edition). Washington, DC, 1998.

NOTES

Preface
  1. Matthew 5:44
  2. Spellman, 5

Chapter 1
  3. Gould, 307
  4. McCallum and Hamblin, 14
  5. Ferris, 290
  6. Job 38:2–7
  7. I Iudson and Corrigan, 45–52

Chapter 2
  8. Churchill, 148–9
  9. Cook, 56
10. Morgan, 458
11. Lancaster, 6
12. Bobrick, 93
13. Lancaster, 64
14. Irving, 147
15. Churchill, 179
16. Lancaster, 93

17. Lancaster, 178

18. Cook, 230

19. Lancaster, 156

20. Declaration of Independence

21. Marshall and Manuel, *The Light and the Glory*, 313

22. Ibid., 315

23. Irving, 324

24. Lancaster, 240

25. Fleming, 427

26. Stryker, 94, 99

27. Ibid., 106

28. Ibid., 107

29. Ibid., 110

30. Ibid., 110–111

31. Fleming, 459; Dwyer, 220

32. Johnson, 53

33. Stryker, 120

34. Fleming, 458; Henderson, 969

35. Irving, 333

36. Wood, 65; Fast, 123; Dwyer, 221

37. Chidsen, 118; Wood, 66; Johnson, 54; Dwyer, 263 cites this story as a "legend"

38. Wallace, 131; Irving, 328

39. Irving, 332

40. Dwyer, 253

41. Lancaster, 246

42. Stember, 30

43. Lancaster, 254

44. Churchill, 191

45. Durant, Will and Ariel, Part X, 922

46. Potter and Nimitz, 90–96

47. Potter and Nimitz, 90

48. Booty, 128; Askew and Spellman, 47

49. Hudson and Corrigan, 90; Askew and Spellman, 42–48

50. Madaras and SoRelle, 86

Chapter 3
51. Hudson and Corrigan, 99
52. Hudson and Corrigan, 133
53. Marshall and Manuel, *Sounding Forth the Trumpet*, 161
54. Lincoln, Vol. IV, 262–71 (First Inaugural Address)
55. Basler, 50
56. Ibid., 75–76
57. Eaton, 36
58. Basler, 21
59. Lincoln, Vol. IV, 262–71
60. Oates, 261
61. Ibid., 268
62. Lincoln, Vol. IV, 48
63. Ibid., Vol. V, 317–18
64. Welles, 242
65. Oates, 241–42
66. Crook, 84
67. Ibid., 58–59
68. Ibid., 86–87
69. Oates, 285
70. Lincoln, Vol. V, 118–25
71. Ibid., 403–4
72. Chase, 411
73. Welles, 248
74. McCabe, 248
75. Ibid., 251
76. Johnson and Buel, 603
77. McClellan, 438
78. Ibid., 453
79. Freeman, Vol. 2, 722
80. Lincoln, Vol. V, 485
81. Catton, 93–104

82. Lincoln, Vol. V, 433–36(Preliminary Emancipation Proclamation)

83. Crook, 97

84. Lincoln, VIII, 332–33 (Second Inaugural Address)

85. Lee, 22

86. Eaton, 69

87. Basler, 35

88. Lee, 23

89. Current, 72

Chapter 4

90. Simons, 30

91. Bocking, 72

92. Leonard, 63

93. Busch, 72

94. Bocking, 77

95. Simons, 39

96. Hart, 104; Spector, 35

97. Hart, 121

98. Morison, 27

99. Fuchida and Okumiya, 32

100. Spector, 82

101. Ibid., 78

102. Morison, 57

103. Spector, 10

104. Fuchida and Okumiya, 69–72

105. Ibid., 59–66

106. Taylor, 49

107. Fuchida and Okumiya, 111

108. Ibid., 112–13

109. Office of Naval Intelligence, 6

110. Fuchida and Okumiya, 133

111. Ibid., 132

112. Sources for action on June 4: Office of Naval Intelligence,

Fuchida and Okumiya, Taylor, Barker, Morison, Potter and Nimitz

113. Office of Naval Intelligence, 7

114. Ibid., 7

115. Bomb damage reports: Office of Naval Intelligence, 8–11; 52–54

116. Spector, 23

117. Bocking, viii

118. Hart, 128

119. Fuchida and Okumiya, 7

120. Farris, 67

121. Ibid., 50

122. Leverton

Chapter 5

123. Churchill, speech at Westminster College, Fulton, MO, March 5, 1946.

124. Askew and Spellman, 195

125. Ibid., 195

126. Ibid., 196–98

127. Parsons, 4

128. Boiter,16

129. Hosking, 237

130. Ibid., 237

131. Boiter, 18

132. Hosking, 440

133. Matthew 5:10

134. Szasc, 89

135. Rhodes, 776–77

136. Bundy, 198

137. Fursenko and Naftali, 14–15, 36. This 1997 work is cited often, as an unbiased source based on recently declassified material.

138. Perez-Stable, 80

139. Fursenko and Naftali, 68

140. Ibid., 71

141. Love, 441

142. Ibid., 442–43

143. Fursenko and Naftali, 125–26,130–31

144. Tompson, 232–35

145. Penkovskiy, 336

146. Love, 445

147. Fursenko and Naftali, 171

148. Tompson, 240; Fursenko and Naftali, 139

149. Fursenko and Naftali, 178

150. Khrushchev, *Khrushchev Remembers*, Talbot, 494

151. Gribkov and Smith, 26–27; Fursenko and Naftali, 187–89. Sources vary slightly on some details of Anadyr forces.

152. Gribkov and Smith, 29

153. Fursenko and Naftali, 197; Hersh, 347

154. *Revelations from the Russian Archives*, 714–15

155. Hersh, 348

156. Love, 448

157. Fursenko and Naftali, 204

158. Tompson, 249

159. Fursenko and Naftali, 210–12

160. Gribkov and Smith, 4–5

161. Fursenko and Naftali, 219

162. Central Intelligence Agency, 140–44, 155

163. Love, 452

164. Kennedy, 39

165. Errickson, 49

166. Love, 453

167. Kennedy, 135–36

168. Beer, 125–26

169. Hersh, 361

170. Beer, 240

171. Ibid., 132, 144

172. Central Intelligence Agency, 304

173. *Revelations from the Russian Archives*, 718

174. Beer, 153; Central Intelligence Agency, 305

175. Beer, 154–57
176. Central Intelligence Agency, 314–16
177. Fursenko and Naftali, 268
178. Gribkov and Smith, 66–67
179. Fursenko and Naftali, 271
180. Ibid., 272–73
181. Gribkov and Smith, 66–67; Fursenko and Naftali, 277–78
182. Allison, 3
183. Kennedy, 107–9
184. Khrushchev, *Glasnost Tapes*, 179
185. Tompson, 253
186. Ibid., 261,272; Hosking, 361
187. Khrushchev, *The Glasnost Tapes*, 176
188. Fursenko and Naftali, 202
189. Bundy, 446
190. Blight and Welch, 348
191. Ibid., 349

Chapter 6
192. Geivett and Habermas, 17
193. Ibid., 103
194. Millman and Childers, 124–27
195. Ibid., 227–31
196. Marshall and Manuel, *The Light and the Glory* and *Sounding Forth the Trumpet*
197. Neiman, 17
198. Ibid., 171
199. Matthew 5:3
200. Bureau of the Census, 72
201. Britannica, 315
202. John 17:25–26
203. John 8:31
204. John 8:36
205. 2 Peter 3:8–9

INDEX